Sue Lawrence

ON SALADS

Sue Lawrence
ON SALADS

With photographs by
GUS FILGATE

KYLE CATHIE LTD

To Bob, my father, with love

Author's Acknowledgements

Thanks to Mary my agent, and to Gus Filgate and Linda Tubby for the photography. Thanks also to Gillian Haslam for editing the book and to Kyle's talented team for all their brilliant ideas.

Special thanks to my family who have had to wade through trug-loads of salads.

First published in Great Britain in 1999 by
Kyle Cathie Limited
20 Vauxhall Bridge Road
London SW1V 2SA

10 9 8 7 6 5 4 3 2 1

ISBN 1 85626 323 1

Edited by Sophie Bessemer
Copy-edited by Gillian Haslam
Designed by Kit Johnson with Dorchester Typesetting Group
Production by Lorraine Baird and Sha Huxtable
Home economy by Linda Tubby

Sue Lawrence is hereby identified as the author of this work in accordance with Section 77 of the Copyright, Designs and Patents Act 1988

A Cataloguing In Publication record for this title is available from the British Library

Colour separations by Chroma Graphics Pte. Ltd., Singapore
Printed and bound in Singapore by Kyodo Printing Co.

CONTENTS

INTRODUCTION

While in Britain we were still placing little crescent-shaped bowls of untossed salad at the top-right corner of each table setting as an accompaniment to our main course, the Americans were devouring their salads before their steak had even arrived. On my first trip to the States I remember thinking how strange it was to be served just a bowl of salad on its own, as a starter. And being asked which salad dressing – Roquefort, Thousand Island, Italian or French – I wanted was a complete novelty. And yet it seemed to me rather a good thing, to get in your greens and a quick blast of health food (which excluded most of their rich, heavy dressings of course) before tucking into the rich, heavy main courses and calorie-laden puddings.

The only other place where I had eaten salad as a separate course was in France. Usually served after the main course, its purpose was to wipe up the meaty or fishy juices, with the help of some morning-fresh baguette. This, too, had seemed strange, and yet the palate-cleansing reason behind this was eminently sensible and the sharp but smooth, oily taste of the mustard-enhanced vinaigrette stayed happily in the mouth throughout the ensuing cheese course.

Well, anything was a contrast to the average British salad of the day: a few slices of cold meat (chopped ham and pork, corned beef – boiled ham if you were lucky), limp lettuce leaves, tired tomato slices and a hillock of black-speckled cress concealing a bleeding circle of vinegary beetroot. If you preferred, there might be a grey-ringed half of hard-boiled egg or a little grated mound of processed orange cheese. Salad cream was served on the side and was meant to swathe the lot – either to disguise the inadequacies of the said ingredients or to add a little sunshine to the plate, depending on how you felt about salad cream.

If, however, you were lucky enough to have a vegetable garden, then things were rather different. Lettuce picked just ten minutes earlier, washed well and then swung round and round in the reliable old plastic salad shaker (I used to be sent running round the garden to shake the lettuce) and tipped onto the plate with the merest suggestion of dressing, was a revelation. As were the freshly pulled spring onions, radishes and, of course, new potatoes. Covered with dirt (now an unknown commodity in supermarket pre-packs), the potatoes would have to be gently scrubbed (not too much for fear of disturbing their all-important skins) then boiled and tossed in butter with perhaps a little mint or parsley. On a sunny summer's day (and was not every summer in childhood filled with sunshine?) there were surely few better things. Followed by bowls of raspberries freshly picked from the canes at the bottom of the garden, it was quite simply sheer bliss.

But childhood memories cannot sustain one forever and so it was in the real world that I was just coming to terms with the anachronistically-placed American salad, the generously dressed French salad, and in particular, with the crescent bowls of my student days working as a waitress in the local restaurant. Fast forward many years and we now have the most incredible array of salad vegetables and fruit available all year round, flown in from all over the globe. To add to our glorious seasonal produce such as lettuce, spinach, sorrel, beetroot, cucumber, peas and all the berries that make up the best of all summer salads, we now have tropical ingredients and those imported from the southern hemisphere to satisfy any out-of-season needs.

Now, wonderful as this all is, I do think it is important to cling to our seasonality and to relish the first exciting bite of jersey potato in early summer. And what about the first time you dip an English asparagus spear into melted butter in spring? And as for the first bite of juicy local raspberry, there is no purer taste of summer. However, we are now lucky to be able to supplement these seasonal joys with mangoes, papayas and sweet potatoes in every month and for any meal. We can whizz up butternut squash in any season for a rich, creamy soup. We can purée imported fresh herbs to make pesto, pistou and salsa, whatever the weather.

One of the joys of all these imported ingredients is that they can be accompaniments to our root vegetables and dried fruits in the winter months. They can be used in the freshest of salads just as we would use our own local produce during spring and summer. As a result, now salads are not only for summer, but for all year round.From January until December, we can enjoy salads warm or cold, designer or plain, main course or starter, meticulously constructed or simply tipped onto the plate. We can even enjoy them for dessert.

We are now more or less on a par with the number of fresh salad ingredients available in the seventeenth century, as outlined in John Evelyn's *Acetaria, A Discourse of Sallets* (1699) where the author lists 73 'Sallet' ingredients from alexanders (similar to celery), cress and fennel to mushrooms, nettles and wood sorrel. Further back in time, the Romans used to eat salad vegetables as a second course accompanied by a seasoned sauce. Cucumbers or endives were dressed with liquamen (a fish-based condiment), lettuces with a spiced vinegary dressing including ginger, cumin and rue.

Although flavour combinations have admittedly changed (another Roman speciality was rose petals, brains and eggs – yum!), there is still ample room for experimentation. And it is with this in mind that I have written this book, to suggest combinations of ingredients that you might not hitherto have considered. Without a doubt, we are eating more and more salads, whether inspired by some fanatical health-kick or simply because we have come to appreciate the fact that they taste so good. To my mind, the main allure of a salad is the fresh taste. If it looks good, of course it is a bonus. So do try to avoid the crescent-shaped little dishes at all costs.

A FRESH START

There is historical evidence why you should begin your meal with a salad rather than having it after the main course. According to John Evelyn in his 1699 book on salads, the Ancients preferred to get the salads out of the way so that they could begin their serious drinking. This is his translation from the Latin:

> 'For if on drinking Wine you lettuce eat,
> It floats upon the Stomach.'

So, if you are feeling the need for more than a glass or two of wine at dinner, it is recommended that you consume your lettuce first for fear of indigestion! Besides, it is a refreshing way to start a meal, whether lunch or dinner, and a genial beginning with family and friends as the salad is slowly shared from a large communal bowl. Bread is torn off at leisure from a large loaf placed in the centre of the table and a dish of butter or bottle of olive oil passed from guest to guest. Starter salads – whether they consist of eggs, cheese, meat, fish or vegetables – are also rather informal and so will set the tone of the meal as casual and convivial.

TUSCAN PANZANELLA

Serves 4–6

2 thick slices of country or
sourdough bread
(at least 2 days old)

3 large (beef) tomatoes, chopped

1/4 red onion, peeled, finely chopped

1/2 cucumber, chopped but unpeeled

2 sticks of celery, chopped

10–12 basil leaves, torn

1 garlic clove, peeled, crushed

Salt and freshly ground
black pepper

6 tablespoons olive oil

2 tablespoons red wine vinegar

Traditionally eaten by shepherds and country folk, fresh-tasting Tuscan salad is hearty and satisfying. It is also a great way to use up leftover bread ... with one proviso. The bread has to be top-quality and preferably Italian country-style or sourdough. Lighter breads will disintegrate. Serve soon after making, so that the bread does not become too soggy. You can embellish this with chopped anchovies or Parmesan shavings.

Tear the bread (thick crusts and all) into large bite-sized chunks and place in a large salad bowl. Top with the tomatoes, onion, cucumber, celery, basil and garlic. Season well with salt and pepper, then slowly pour over the oil and vinegar. Toss well together so that the bread is soaked, but take care you do not break up the bread. (I use two very large spoons to do this.) Check the seasoning and serve with plenty of the juices.

SALAD PICNIC LOAF

Serves 6–8

1 ciabatta

4 tablespoons extra virgin olive oil

3 tablespoons pesto or tapenade
(see page 156)

150g (5½oz) Mozzarella cheese
(preferably buffalo), sliced

150g (5½oz) feta cheese, sliced

Large handful each of rocket, baby
spinach and iceberg, washed, dried,
roughly chopped

2 large tomatoes, sliced

2 tablespoons basil leaves

Vary this delicious picnic loaf by using a sourdough or granary loaf and substitute other salad leaves for those listed.

Slice the loaf horizontally and remove some of the soft bread to make room for the filling. Brush both inside halves with 3 tablespoons oil. Spread the pesto or tapenade over both sides.

Layer the sliced cheese, salad leaves, tomatoes and basil on one half, seasoning generously with salt and pepper as you go. Drizzle with the remaining tablespoon of oil, top with the other half loaf and wrap firmly in double foil.

Refrigerate overnight, then remove and cut into thick slices with an extremely sharp knife.

MUSHROOM SALAD WITH BALSAMIC DRESSING

Serves 3–4

450g (1lb) large mushrooms, wiped

4 tablespoons olive oil

1 tablespoon fresh oregano leaves

Salt and freshly ground
black pepper

1 tablespoon balsamic vinegar

Before my stay in Finland – home of great wild mushroom pickers and yummy mushroom salad recipes – the only time I had ever eaten mushrooms cold was in that 1960s' and 70s' stalwart 'champignons à la grecque'. I can't explain why, but I used to detest them. Perhaps it was their rubbery texture or the dried herbs adhering to them, but I used to baulk when I saw them. Over the years, however, my prejudice against cold mushrooms has waned and now I positively enjoy them, provided they are served in an interesting and fresh-tasting dressing. Thank goodness dried herbs have been more or less banished from use in favour of fresh.

Thickly slice the mushrooms. Heat the oil in a frying pan, add the mushrooms and cook for about 10 minutes until tender. Then tip the mushrooms into a salad bowl and allow to cool. Roughly tear the oregano leaves and add them to the mushrooms, with a good grinding of salt and pepper and the balsamic vinegar. Serve at room temperature with fresh bread for dipping.

MOLTEN CHEESE & REDCURRANT SALAD

Serves 6

1 cos lettuce, washed, roughly cut

2 heads of chicory

Salt and freshly ground
black pepper

140 g (5 oz) redcurrants, removed
from their stalks

200 g (7 oz) Camembert-style cheese
(this is the weight with the rind on)

75 ml (3 fl oz) dry white wine

75 ml (3 fl oz) double cream

2 handfuls of croûtons (optional)
(see page 20)

This warm salad can be made with various cheeses. I always used Bonchester, that rich, creamy cheese from the Scottish Borders, until it was sadly withdrawn from production in 1998. However, any Camembert-style cheese, such as Cooleney, made in Tipperary, Ireland, makes a good substitute, as does French Reblochon or Italian Fontina.

Place the cos and chicory in a bowl and season the leaves. Tip over the currants.

Cut the rind from the cheese and chop roughly. Place in a small saucepan with the wine and cream. Over a very low heat, heat very gently, stirring, until the cheese is melted. Do not boil. Season with salt and pepper to taste. Pour the dressing all over the salad and top with croûtons, if using. Serve at once.

BARBECUED CAMEMBERT WITH CRUDITÉS

Serves 6–8

1 whole Camembert cheese, about
300 g (10½ oz)

Carrot sticks, chicory leaves, tiny
broccoli spears, celery and fennel
sticks, cucumber batons, for
dunking

If you want to make this outside the all-too-short barbecue season, just place it in a medium-hot oven. Instead of the vegetable dippers, you can use chunks of apple or pear instead: dip them in lemon juice to stop discolouring.

Remove the cheese from its packaging and double wrap in foil. Place on a preheated barbecue for 3–5 minutes on each side. Test it is ready by gently pressing in the middle: it should feel soft and gooey.

To serve, place on a plate and unwrap the foil. Dunk in the crudités while it is still warm and molten.

ROQUEFORT & WALNUT SALAD

Serves 4

2 heads of chicory

1 frisée lettuce, washed

75g (2¾oz) Roquefort cheese, crumbled

3 tablespoons natural yoghurt

¼ red onion, peeled, very finely chopped

The juice of 1 lemon

Freshly ground black pepper

50g (1¾oz) walnuts, chopped

A handful of seedless green grapes

You could use another blue cheese for this recipe – Lanark Blue would be ideal, as it is also made from ewe's milk and has the same softish, rather crumbly texture. With a firmer blue cheese, you may need to alter the amount of lemon juice or yoghurt, to give the correct creamy texture for the dressing. Serve this salad with warm soda bread for a substantial starter.

Cut the chicory into large pieces and place in a salad bowl with the frisée.

Place the cheese, yoghurt, onion and lemon juice in a food processor and whizz until blended, then add pepper to taste. Just before serving, pour this over the salad. Top with the nuts and grapes and take to the table. Toss at the table and serve with soda bread.

WARM PAPPARDELLE & ROCKET PESTO SALAD

Serves 4

75g (2¾oz) rocket

100g (3½oz) shelled nuts

55g (2oz) Parmesan cheese, freshly grated, plus shavings to serve

Approximately 5 tablespoons extra virgin olive oil plus extra

Salt and freshly ground black pepper

350g (12oz) pappardelle, freshly cooked and drained

Use any sort of nut (hazelnuts, walnuts, pecans, brazils, pistachios) you happen to have in your larder, provided they are fresh: don't forget nuts become rancid fairly quickly.

To make the pesto, place the rocket, nuts, cheese and oil in a food processor and whizz until blended, adding salt and pepper to taste.

Add about 3 heaped tablespoons of the pesto into the warm, drained pasta and toss gently, adding an extra tablespoon of oil if it seems too thick. Cool and serve drizzled with a little extra oil. Garnish with some Parmesan shavings.

AUBERGINE & MUSTARD SALAD

Serves 4

1 large aubergine, wiped, cut into large dice

5 tablespoons olive oil

Mixed salad leaves, washed

3 teaspoons wholegrain mustard

1 teaspoon runny honey

The juice of half a lemon

Salt and freshly ground black pepper

If you can get hold of red mustard leaves, do use them, as their mustard flavour obviously marries perfectly with the dressing. Otherwise, use a peppery leaf such as rocket or watercress.

Preheat the oven to 200°C/400°F/gas mark 6.

Place the aubergine chunks in a roasting tin and pour over 2 tablespoons of the oil. Place in the oven and roast for about 45 minutes, stirring gently twice, so the aubergine does not stick to the tin.

Place the salad leaves in a generous salad bowl. To make the dressing, whisk together the mustard, the remaining oil, honey and lemon juice. Season to taste with a good grinding of salt and pepper.

Once the aubergines are cooked, allow them to cool, occasionally stirring them carefully so they do not stick, then tip them over the salad leaves and toss in the mustard dressing. Serve at once.

EGG & SORREL MAYONNAISE

Serves 4

4 large free-range eggs

55g (2oz) young sorrel

2 medium free-range egg yolks

½ teaspoon Dijon mustard

½ teaspoon salt

150ml (5fl oz) sunflower oil

100ml (3½fl oz) extra virgin olive oil

Freshly ground mixed peppercorns (optional)

Round lettuce leaves, washed

Remember Egg Mayonnaise? It was one of those ubiquitous starters in the 1960s and 70s and was invariably a plate of grey-tinged egg under a mantle of dubious mayo, which strangely enough often seemed to emanate from a bottle of salad cream... or at least it did in the restaurant where I waitressed. It was by no means a dish likely to provoke odes of joy. But, when well-executed, it is a lovely dish worth rediscovering, especially when the mayonnaise is flavoured with that wonderfully fresh spring herb, sorrel. Serve this with sliced brown bread and butter.

Place the eggs in a pan of cold water then bring to the boil. Once boiling, cook for 6–7 minutes, then remove and place immediately under cold running water. Leave them there for at least 1 minute, to stop them cooking further.

For the mayonnaise, place the sorrel, egg yolks, mustard and salt in a food processor. Process for a few seconds, just until the sorrel is chopped.

Place the oils in a reliable jug, i.e. one that pours easily without sloshing its contents all in at once. Then, with the machine running, add the oil drop by drop – this is crucial, otherwise the mixture will curdle. Once you have dribbled in about a quarter of the oil, increase the drip to a thin stream, and continue until all the oil has been added. You should have a thick, glossy, green-flecked mayonnaise. Taste for seasoning and add ground peppercorns if necessary. (If by any chance the mayonnaise has curdled, do not throw it away; try adding an ice-cube and processing it again.)

To serve, peel the eggs, then cut in half. Place some lettuce on each plate, then two egg halves on top. Spoon over some of the luscious mayo and serve. Listen out for tales of 'I remember the egg mayonnaise I used to eat 20 or 30 years ago'. Just nod demurely.

GUACAMOLE WITH BLUE CORN CHIPS

Serves 3–4

1 large ripe avocado, peeled, roughly chopped

1 plum tomato, peeled, seeded, diced

½ red chilli, finely chopped

The juice of 1 lime

1 tablespoon freshly chopped coriander

Salt and freshly ground black pepper

Blue corn chips, to serve

Traditionally this wonderful dip is made in the Mexican 'molcajete' (mortar) with a 'tejolete' (pestle). It should never be made in a food processor. You do not want a smooth, globby purée, but a soft, rough-textured mixture. Usually served at the beginning of a meal with a pile of hot, freshly made tortillas or crisply fried pork skins, it also accompanies dishes such as tacos, enchiladas and quesadillas. If you can only find unripe avocados, place them in a paper bag with a banana. This gives off ethylene gas which speeds their ripening.

Serve the guacamole with a pile of blue corn chips made from a special variety of blue corn. These are widely available in supermarkets but, if you cannot find any, regular corn chips will be just as good.

Place the avocado in a bowl with the tomato, chilli, lime juice and coriander and mix. Season with salt and pepper to taste. Serve in a bowl accompanied by blue corn chips.

ROASTED SQUASH WITH BLUE CHEESE DRESSING

Serves 4

Approximately 900g (2 lb) squash, peeled, deseeded, cut into cubes about 2.5 cm (1 inch) square

3 tablespoons olive oil

2 thick slices of white bread, cubed

Mixed salad leaves

Blue Cheese dressing (see page 157)

Use either butternut squash or acorn squash for this salad. And be sure to arm yourself with a very sharp knife before attempting to cut and peel the squash.

Preheat the oven to 220°C/400°F/gas mark 6. Place the squash on a baking tray with 2 tablespoons of oil and roast for about 45 minutes, or until golden brown and tender. Fry the bread in the remaining oil until crispy.

Place the salad leaves in a bowl, top with the squash and croûtons and drizzle over the Blue Cheese dressing. Serve at once, while the squash and croûtons are still warm.

RATATOUILLE SALAD

Serves 8

450g (1 lb) courgettes, cut into rounds

2 red peppers, chopped

2 aubergines, cut into thick slices

3 large garlic cloves, whole but peeled

1 red onion, peeled, cut into quarters

2 large (beef) tomatoes, cut into eighths

5–6 tablespoons olive oil

Salt and freshly ground black pepper

1 tablespoon red wine vinegar

Vegetables retain more of their texture when cooked in the oven rather than a saucepan and are less prone to disintegrating into the sloppy mush which is sadly the fate of some so-called ratatouilles. In theory, the vegetables should be cooked separately in different pans, but this oven method ensures they still have plenty of bite. Use the best olive oil you can afford to dress this – preferably from Provence, where this legendary dish is everyday fare. Serve with plenty of baguette or, if you have time, make some bread of your own and stud it with some tiny Niçoise olives and scatter over some 'herbes de Provence' just before baking.

Preheat the oven to 240°C/475°F/gas mark 9. Place the courgettes, peppers, aubergines, garlic, onion and tomatoes in a large (or two smaller) roasting tin and drizzle over 2–3 tablespoons of oil. Season well with salt and pepper and cook for about half an hour, or until the vegetables are tinged golden brown and are tender.

Mix 3 tablespoons of oil, the vinegar and plenty of salt and pepper together.

Carefully lift the vegetables onto a shallow serving dish and pour over any juices. Slowly pour over the dressing and toss very gently. Serve at room temperature.

HERB SALAD IN A PARMESAN BASKET

Serves 4

FOR THE PARMESAN BASKETS

100g (3½oz) plain flour, sifted

100g (3½oz) freshly grated Parmesan cheese

100g (3½oz) unsalted butter, diced

1 medium egg, beaten

FOR THE SALAD

Rocket, watercress, young spinach, washed

½ tablespoon of each herb, torn

1 large garlic clove, peeled, crushed

3 tablespoons sunflower oil

1 tablespoon raspberry vinegar

¼ teaspoon mustard

Handful of nasturtiums or other edible flowers (optional)

For the herbs, use four or five from the following list: chervil, basil, flat-leaf parsley, mint, tarragon, marjoram, chives. Excess pastry can be rolled into a log shape and chilled, wrapped in clingfilm. Then cut into 8–10 thin discs and place on a buttered baking tray. Bake at the same temperature as the tarts for 10–15 minutes, or until cooked through. Serve with drinks.

For the parmesan pastry, place the flour, Parmesan and butter in a food processor and whizz briefly, then add the beaten egg and 1 tablespoon of cold water through the feeder tube. Process briefly, then gather together with your hands into a ball. Wrap in clingfilm and chill for about 1 hour. Then roll out to fit four 10cm (4in) loose-bottom tart tins. Prick the bases and chill for at least 2 hours, preferably overnight.

Preheat the oven to 200°C/400°F/gas mark 6. Fill each tart with a sheet of foil and some baking beans and bake for 15 minutes, then remove the foil and beans and cook for a further 5–10 minutes until cooked through. Remove and leave to cool, but do not refrigerate.

For the salad, place the salad leaves in a bowl, then top with the torn herbs. Place the garlic, oil, vinegar and mustard in a screw-top jar and shake well. Pour over the salad and toss well.

To serve, remove each tart from its tin and place on a plate. Fill with a light pile of the herb salad and then, if you like, add a flower or two. Serve at once.

GREEK FETA, OLIVE & COURGETTE SALAD

Serves 6

3 large courgettes, cut into 4–5 slices horizontally

3 tablespoons olive oil

100g (3½oz) feta cheese, crumbled

12–18 kalamata olives, stoned

1 heaped tablespoon fresh oregano, roughly torn

Freshly ground black pepper

I have specifically labelled this dish 'Greek feta' as I believe Greek to be the best (Cypriot is also good). I really do not rate French feta at all, as its rather neutral flavour does not compare with the lovely crumbly texture and salty, punchy flavour of real ewes' and goats' milk feta made in Greece. Serve this salad with warm pitta or any other flat bread.

Place the courgette slices on a sheet of foil and brush with some of the oil. Place under a hot grill and grill for about 10 minutes, turning, or until golden brown and tender. Remove and cool, then place in a shallow dish. Scatter over the crumbled feta, then the olives and finally the oregano. Season with plenty of pepper (not salt as feta is such a salty cheese). Drizzle over the remaining oil and serve at room temperature.

SPINACH WITH YOGHURT & DILL

Serves 6

25g (1oz) pine nuts

200g (7oz) young spinach, washed

4 heaped tablespoons natural yoghurt (preferably Greek)

The juice of 1 large lemon

3 heaped tablespoons freshly chopped dill

1 garlic clove, peeled, crushed

Salt and freshly ground black pepper

A Turkish-inspired salad, this is light, refreshing and definitely one for the summer months. I used to eat this salad made with purslane which has round fleshy stalks and leaves. Popular in Greece, Turkey and the Middle East, it is difficult to obtain here so I suggest using young spinach instead.

First, toast the pine nuts. Place them on a sheet of foil under a preheated grill. Toast for 2–3 minutes, turning once. They can burn very quickly so keep a close eye on them.

Place the spinach in a bowl. Stir together the yoghurt, lemon juice, dill, garlic and plenty of salt and pepper. Toss through the spinach, then scatter over the pine nuts just before serving.

POLENTA CROÛTON, TOMATO & PESTO SALAD

Serves 6–8

500g (1lb 2oz) cooked polenta

2 tablespoons olive oil, for frying

3–4 large tomatoes, sliced

1 heaped tablespoon pesto
(see page 156)

3 tablespoons extra virgin olive oil

Salt and freshly ground
black pepper

It is now possible to buy packets of polenta that has already been cooked. If, however, you cannot find any, just cook the polenta according to packet instructions (usually 2 litres/3½ pints of water for a 375g/13oz packet), then pour into a shallow dish and cool.

Cut the polenta into cubes (croûton-size). Heat the olive oil in a frying pan and fry the croûtons for about 5 minutes until golden brown and crispy, turning frequently. Drain on kitchen paper.

Meanwhile, lay the tomatoes on a shallow serving plate. Mix together the pesto, extra virgin oil, salt and pepper and pour over the tomatoes. Scatter over the polenta croûtons and serve at once.

PEAR, PECAN & SPINACH SALAD WITH POPPYSEED DRESSING

Serves 4

200g (7oz) young spinach, washed

2 large dessert pears, cut into slices

100g (3½oz) shelled pecan nuts

1 tablespoon poppyseeds

1 teaspoon Dijon mustard

3 tablespoons olive oil

1 tablespoon raspberry vinegar

Salt and freshly ground
black pepper

Toasting the nuts adds a deeper flavour to the entire dish: place them on a sheet of foil and place under a preheated grill for 3–4 minutes, turning often, until a light golden brown. Watch carefully as they tend to burn quickly. Serve this with lots of warm, fresh bread.

Place the spinach in a salad bowl, add the pears and nuts and combine together. Whisk together the remaining ingredients, season to taste and pour the dressing over the salad. Serve at once.

Goats' Cheese & Beetroot Salad

Serves 4

200g (7oz) firm goats' cheese, cut into large cubes, about 2cm (¾in) square

75g (2¾oz) unsalted butter, melted

65g (2½oz) fresh brown breadcrumbs, seasoned with salt and pepper

110g (4oz) cooked beetroot, cubed (same size as cheese)

Large bag of baby spinach

Vinaigrette (see page 154)

This is based on a delicious salad I enjoyed in a tiny fishing village in the archipelago near Stockholm. Having had my fill of herring, I opted for a cheesy starter instead. It was a large croûte of bread topped with thick rings of beetroot, with a gooey slice of molten goats' cheese on top. My recipe is far simpler, yet no less delicious. Serve with Swedish rye or pumpernickel bread.

Toss the cheese in half the butter then add the breadcrumbs, shaking gently to coat all over. Chill for an hour or so.

Heat the remaining butter in a non-stick frying pan and fry the cheese briefly until golden brown.

Combine the beetroot and spinach in a bowl, toss in some Vinaigrette, then top with the crisply fried cheese. Serve with bread and eat at once.

CAULIFLOWER & GUACAMOLE SALAD

Serves 4

4 mini cauliflowers, trimmed

1 large ripe avocado

3–4 spring onions, finely chopped

½–1 green chilli, deseeded, finely chopped

The juice of 1 lemon

1 tablespoon freshly chopped coriander

Salt and freshly ground black pepper

2 large tomatoes, sliced

Yet another simple salad, which looks terrific with its colours of green and white. Serve on its own or as part of a buffet table.

First boil the cauliflowers until just tender, then plunge in cold water and drain well.

Chop the avocado and mix in a bowl with the onions, chilli, lemon juice and coriander. Season to taste with salt and pepper. (Remember that authentic Mexican guacamole is never made in a food processor – it should be roughly mashed, not a smooth, homogenous mess.)

To serve, place the cauliflowers on a shallow serving dish. Surround each cauliflower – or the whole dish – with the tomato slices, then spoon the guacamole over the tops of each cauli. Serve at room temperature.

AVOCADO WITH WALNUTS

Serves 4

2 large ripe avocados, peeled, sliced

The juice of 1 lemon

50g (1¾oz) walnuts, shelled

2 tablespoons walnut oil

Salt and freshly ground black pepper

I have always loved walnut oil drizzled over avocados. This simple salad is just an extension of this, and can be embellished if you wish with chopped red onions or some fresh herbs. But I like to eat it just as it is. Serve soon after making with fresh bread, preferably walnut.

Arrange the avocado slices on a shallow serving plate and squeeze over the lemon juice. Scatter over the nuts, drizzle the oil over the top and season well with salt and pepper.

CAPRESE STACK WITH PARSLEY SALSA

Serves 4

4 large (beef) tomatoes

12 slices about 298g (10½oz)
Mozzarella cheese
(preferably buffalo)

Salt and freshly ground
black pepper

Large bunch of basil leaves

15g (½oz) flat-leaf parsley

1 tablespoon capers, drained

1 heaped teaspoon Dijon mustard

3–4 anchovy fillets, drained

4 tablespoons extra virgin olive oil

'Caprese' is the name of a much-loved Italian salad of tomatoes, Mozzarella and basil. It is served here as a towering pile or stack and drizzled with a parsley salsa which not only makes it look good, but also adds an interesting savoury tang. Be sure to bring the cheese to room temperature long before serving – there is nothing worse than cold cheese.

Cut each tomato into 4 slices. To assemble the stack, place a tomato slice in the centre of a plate, top with a slice of cheese, then season with salt and pepper and place a basil leaf on top. Continue the layers, using four slices of tomato and three of cheese per person, ending with a tomato slice.

Place the parsley, about 8–10 basil leaves, the capers, mustard and anchovies in a food processor and process until blended, then pour in the oil, season to taste and mix together well.

To serve, spoon over a generous amount of the parsley salsa over the top of each stack and serve with plenty of fresh ciabatta bread.

ROASTED FENNEL WITH STILTON

Serves 4

2 large fennel bulbs, trimmed

4 tablespoons extra virgin olive oil

100g (3½oz) Stilton cheese, crumbled

Salt and freshly ground black pepper

This is one of those salads that are exceedingly handy to serve at supper or dinner parties, as it can be fully prepared well in advance. The fennel can be roasted in the morning, then, once cool, topped with the cheese and left for several hours, to allow the flavours to fuse together. You might not think that a salad of two ingredients would be earth-shatteringly exciting, but, because of the strength of flavours, this one (in my humble opinion) is.

Preheat the oven to 230°C/450°F/gas mark 8. Cut the fennel into quarters and remove any hard core. Place the pieces in an ovenproof dish and drizzle over the oil and plenty of salt and pepper. Roast in the oven for 30–35 minutes, or until tender, turning once. Remove the fennel from the dish and allow to cool thoroughly. Allow the oil to cool and set aside for serving.

Arrange the fennel in a serving dish and spoon over the oil. Crumble over the cheese and leave at room temperature until ready to serve.

SHREDDED OMELETTE WITH GHERKINS

Serves 3–4

3 large free-range eggs

Salt and freshly ground
black pepper

15g (½oz) unsalted butter

4–5 gherkins, sliced

4–5 spring onions, chopped

2 plump heads of chicory, sliced

3 tablespoons olive oil

1 tablespoon balsamic vinegar

First you have to learn how to make the perfect omelette. And there is no such thing as a perfect omelette without the perfect pan. So if you do not possess a reliable omelette pan (non-stick is not actually recommended here), then consider the alternative: a lifetime without omelettes. If this does not impel you to go out and buy one, then stop reading this recipe right now. I use my ancient and exceedingly heavy cast-iron pan, but some swear by aluminium pans. It is also crucial, if you are serving the omelette hot, to slightly undercook it as it will continue to cook even on the plate. However, for this recipe (where the omelette is cut into slivers and served cold), it should be cooked slightly beyond the soft, squidgy stage.

To make the omelette, beat the eggs lightly in a bowl with salt and pepper. Melt the butter in the pan and, once the butter bubbles and hisses a little, pour in the eggs. Do not touch for at least 30 seconds then, using a spatula, keep flicking the soft inners towards the edges, which should have lightly set. Keep tilting the pan as you do this. Aim to shift the set edges into the middle and to ease the liquid eggs towards the edges. After no more than 2 minutes the omelette is ready, so flip it over and slide onto a plate. However, for this recipe, leave it for perhaps another 20 seconds or so, then flip over and slide onto a board. When completely cold, cut into slivers.

Mix the gherkins, spring onions and chicory together in a bowl. Stir together the oil, vinegar and salt and pepper and dress the salad, tossing well. Place the omelette slices on top and serve at once.

GOATS' CHEESE CROÛTON & TARRAGON SALAD

Serves 4

8 slices of 'ficelle'
(narrow baguette)

8 slices of goats' cheese
(roughly the same diameter as
the bread slices)

4 tablespoons olive oil

1 tablespoon tarragon vinegar

1 tablespoon freshly
chopped tarragon, plus a
few sprigs to garnish

1 teaspoon Dijon mustard

Salt and freshly ground
black pepper

Rocket, frisée or baby spinach,
washed

These are little croûtes of melted goats' cheese topping a tarragon-flavoured salad. Use a firm goats' cheese, ideally cut from a log ('bûche') or a 'crottin'. Use 'Crottin de Chavignol' if you want a pungent flavour – and a decidedly lingering after-taste.

Preheat the oven to 190°C/375°F/gas mark 5. Place the bread slices on a baking tray. Top each with a slice of cheese, then drizzle 1 tablespoon of oil over the tops. Bake for about 10 minutes, or until the cheese is melted.

Meanwhile, mix the remaining oil with the vinegar, tarragon, mustard and salt and pepper. Place the salad leaves in a bowl and toss in the dressing. Top with the cheese croûtons and serve at once.

MIDDLE-EASTERN FATTOUSH

Serves 6

2 large pitta breads

½ cucumber, diced

2 large tomatoes, chopped

4 spring onions, chopped

Salt and freshly ground
black pepper

2 heaped tablespoons
flat-leaf parsley

2 heaped tablespoons mint

2 heaped teaspoons coriander

4 tablespoons olive oil

The juice of 1 lemon

This is an extremely popular Middle-Eastern salad, particularly loved in Lebanon and Syria. It is important to grill the pitta bread really well until it is crisp and golden brown. If it is not completely crisp, it will soon become soggy when mixed with the other ingredients. The choice of herbs is of course up to you, but I suggest mint, flat parsley and coriander for true authenticity. If you can find any purslane, tear some of this in too. Be sure to serve this salad soon after mixing.

Split the pitta in half by carefully cutting it open with a sharp knife. Toast the four halves under a hot grill until crispy and golden brown all over. Then roughly tear into bite-sized chunks and place in a salad bowl.

Add the cucumber, tomatoes and spring onions with plenty of salt and pepper. Roughly tear the herbs and add, along with the oil and lemon juice. Stir well, check the seasoning and serve immediately.

LENTILS & SALT COD

Serves 8

450g (1 lb) salt cod

2 tablespoons olive oil

1 teaspoon freshly chopped
young rosemary

250g (9 oz) puy lentils

2 tablespoons walnut oil

The juice of 1 lemon

4–5 tomatoes, chopped

3 tablespoons flat-leaf parsley

Salt and freshly ground
black pepper

This is a Catalan-inspired recipe. In north-eastern Spain 'bacalla' is served with tomato sauce, peppers, spinach or even honey. Little tapas of potato and salt cod fritters are served in Catalonian bars. In Provence it is made into the famous 'brandade de morue', a delicious salt cod and potato purée sometimes flavoured with walnut oil instead of olive oil. Clarissa Dickson Wright in her book Two Fat Ladies *also tells of a Caribbean dish of salt cod fishcakes (which she serves with a red pepper tapenade) – saltfish, she writes, has been a mainstay of Barbados since the days of eighteenth-century slavery.*

So, here is my version of a simple Catalan salad – it is salt cod served on a bed of lentils that have been dressed in walnut oil and plenty of fresh parsley. Do be sure to soak the salt cod well. Some take at least 48 hours, depending on the salting procedure. The salt cod I buy from my fishmonger has not been as heavily salted as some Mediterranean cooks like it, and so needs only 24 hours de-salinating. Remember that it is essential to keep changing the water at regular intervals.

First, soak the cod in cold water for at least 24 hours, depending on how heavily it has been salted. Change the water as often as possible. Then pat thoroughly dry and, using a sharp knife, cut at an angle, so you have thin slices, rather like smoked salmon. Place these on a plate and drizzle with the olive oil and the rosemary. Clingwrap and leave in the refrigerator for at least 2 hours.

Cook the lentils according to the packet's instructions, then drain well. Stir in the walnut oil, lemon juice, tomatoes, parsley and salt and pepper.

To serve, place the lentils and dressing in a shallow dish, then top with the salt cod. Grind over plenty of black pepper (no salt) and serve at room temperature.

CLASSIC SALADE NIÇOISE

Serves 4–6

1 cos lettuce, washed

200 g (7 oz) small waxy potatoes, scrubbed

100 g (3½ oz) thin French beans, trimmed

4 tablespoons Provençal olive oil

1 tablespoon red wine vinegar

1 garlic clove, peeled, chopped

½ teaspoon Dijon mustard

Salt and freshly ground black pepper

3 hard-boiled free-range eggs, quartered

3 plum tomatoes, quartered

200 g (7 oz) tin tuna, drained

50 g (1¾ oz) tin anchovies, drained

10–12 black olives, stoned

Salade Niçoise is one of simplest of all salads and, when properly made, can be one of the most memorable. Although people disagree over the inclusion of beans, potatoes and even canned tuna (some purists insist that anchovies should be the only fish), this is more or less the classic version that you are likely to find in Provence. It was a great favourite of mine when I lived there – in fact it marked the beginning of my love affair with olives. Until then I had avoided them like the plague. In a Salade Niçoise they are such an integral part that I ate them at first politely, and finally with relish.

Tear the lettuce into a salad bowl.

Boil the potatoes until tender, then drain and set aside. Boil the beans until just tender, then plunge into cold water. Pat dry and cool.

Whisk together the oil, vinegar, garlic, mustard and salt and pepper, then pour all over the lettuce. Toss well.

Arrange the potatoes and beans with the eggs and tomatoes on top of the lettuce, then top with the tuna, anchovies and olives (criss-crossing the anchovies and olives if you wish to be artistic). Serve with plenty of fresh baguettes or 'pain de campagne'.

SALADE NIÇOISE WITH PEPPERED TUNA STEAK

Serves 4

1–2 tablespoons black peppercorns, cracked or very coarsely ground

500g (1 lb 2oz) fresh tuna steak, cut into 4 pieces

4 tablespoons olive oil

1 cos lettuce, washed

Salt and freshly ground black pepper

125g (4½oz) fine green beans, blanched

4 tomatoes, quartered

2 hard-boiled free-range eggs, quartered

1 tablespoon red wine vinegar

8–10 anchovy fillets, shredded

16–20 black olives, stoned

This is my variation on the Salade Niçoise. The principle of peppering the tuna is the same for beef in 'steak au poivre'. If you do not want to serve the peppered tuna with the salad, you can serve it with a reduced sauce, as you would serve 'steak au poivre', but omit the cream and brandy. Just remove the cooked tuna steaks from the pan, then add a glass of red wine to the pan, reduce down, season and serve this over the tuna, with some green vegetables and new potatoes on the side.

Scatter the peppercorns on a plate or work surface. Brush the tuna with 1 tablespoon of oil, then press into the peppercorns to coat all over. Set aside while you make the salad.

Tear the cos into a large bowl and season with salt and pepper. Top with the beans, tomatoes and eggs.

Heat the remaining oil in a frying pan and, once it is hot, add the tuna and fry for about 3 minutes on each side until cooked; do not overcook or it will be dry. Tip the tuna and the oil over the salad, then return the pan to the heat. Add the vinegar, stir for a few seconds and pour this over the tuna. Top with the anchovy fillets and olives and serve at once.

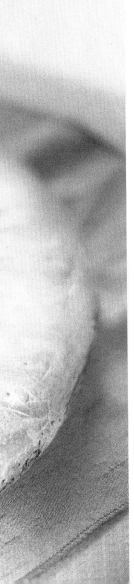

ORIENTAL NOODLE SALAD

Serves 6

250g (9oz) dried Chinese noodles

1 tablespoon freshly grated root ginger

5 tablespoons sunflower oil

The juice of 1 large lime

1 tablespoon soy sauce

Dash of chilli sauce (optional)

Salt and freshly ground black pepper

300g (10½oz) cooked cockles, prawns or clams, shelled

1 large mango, diced

3 tablespoons freshly chopped coriander

3–4 spring onions, chopped

This is one of those wonderful recipes that you can add to as you please, depending on the supplies you have in your refrigerator and freezer. I love to use cockles for this (un-oriental as they are!) but if you prefer prawns or clams, then these also work well. A mixture of all three is best of all.

Cook the noodles according to the packet's instructions, then drain. Mix together the ginger, oil, lime juice, soy and chilli sauce if using, and season to taste. Pour over the noodles, tossing well to coat.

When cool, add the remaining ingredients and toss again. Serve at room temperature.

ROCKET, ARTICHOKE & PANCETTA SALAD

Serves 6

100g (3½oz) rocket, washed

Salt and freshly ground
black pepper

300g (10½oz) jar of char-grilled
artichokes in olive oil

75g (2¾oz) Parmesan cheese,
coarsely grated

100g (3½oz) pancetta, very thinly
sliced (not thickly diced)

1 tablespoon balsamic vinegar

Try to find char-grilled artichokes for the very best flavour. Use ones that have been preserved in extra virgin olive oil and use the oil for the dressing. The pancetta (Italian belly pork) adds both a contrasting crunchy texture and a contrast of heat – once the salad has been tossed it should be served immediately, while the pancetta is still warm. So, when you begin frying, call wayward guests to your table.

Place the rocket in a bowl and season with salt and pepper.

Drain and roughly chop the artichokes, then place on top. Scatter over the Parmesan. Make a dressing by whisking together half the olive oil from the jar with the vinegar.

Meanwhile, fry the pancetta slices in a large non-stick pan (without fat) for about 4–5 minutes, or until crispy. Tip the contents of the pan over the salad. Add the dressing and toss everything together well. Serve at once.

PENNE WITH PESTO & BEEF

Serves 6

500g (1lb 2oz) penne

2 heaped tablespoons pesto
(see page 156)

1 tablespoon olive oil

Salt and freshly ground
black pepper

200g (7oz) sliced rare beef, cut into
slivers

Fresh basil sprigs, to serve

Leftover rare roast beef is best for this recipe; otherwise, you can fry a couple of small thick fillet steaks until rare, cool then slice.

Cook the pasta, then drain well. Toss in the pesto and oil and season to taste with salt and pepper. Cool to room temperature, then toss in the beef.

Check the seasoning again and add a little extra oil if it is rather solid. Garnish with a sprig or two of basil and serve in individual bowls.

Danish Gypsy Salad

Serves 4–6

150 g (5½ oz) small Jersey new
potatoes, scrubbed

100 g (3½ oz) Havarti cheese, cubed

100 g (3½ oz) salami, preferably
peppered, chopped

2 sticks of celery, chopped

50 g (1¾ oz) cooked peas

3 tablespoons mayonnaise
(see page 154)

1 rounded teaspoon Dijon mustard

Pinch of paprika

Salt and freshly ground
black pepper

*Salads play an important role in the Danish way of eating and
are often highlights of the typical 'Smorrebrod', or Cold Table.
Potatoes are widely used in salads and usually, as in other
Scandinavian countries, they are cooked unpeeled then skinned
afterwards. I recommend Jersey new potatoes for this salad as
their flavour is hard to beat. Havarti cheese is a Danish semi-soft
cows' milk cheese which is full flavoured when young, with the
flavour increasing as it matures.*

Boil the potatoes until just tender, then drain. While still
warm, in a bowl combine the potatoes with the remaining
ingredients and add salt and pepper to taste. Serve either
warm or at room temperature, but never cold.

Frisée & Bacon Salad

Serves 4

1 frisée lettuce, washed

1 shallot, peeled, finely chopped

Salt and freshly ground
black pepper

3 tablespoons olive oil

250 g (9 oz) smoked streaky dry-cure
bacon, diced

1 tablespoon red wine vinegar

*It is important to use a dry-cure bacon for this simple salad. If
you don't, there will most likely be a milky-white goo exuding
from your pan instead of lovely bacon fat. And since you pour
the contents of the pan over the lettuce, this is not to be
recommended.*

Place the frisée in a bowl and toss with the shallot and
plenty of salt and pepper.

Heat the oil in a frying pan until hot, then fry the bacon
until crispy and brown. Once the cubes are golden brown,
add the vinegar, stir for a few seconds, then pour the
contents of the pan over the salad. Toss and serve at once.

FRIED QUAILS' EGG & BACON SALAD

Serves 4

1 cos lettuce, washed, shredded

1 frisée, washed, shredded

Salt and freshly ground
black pepper

4 tablespoons extra virgin olive oil

8 slices smoked bacon, diced

8 quails' eggs

1 tablespoon sherry vinegar

For some strange reason, people are rather wary of cooking quails' eggs. This is possibly because they have tried – once – to hard-boil them, then spent absolutely ages trying to peel them without the egg white coming away with the shell. It can be a tiresome task. But frying them is a doddle. Try them instead of fried hens' eggs for breakfast.

Place the lettuce and frisée in a bowl and season with salt and pepper.

Place 3 tablespoons of oil in a frying pan and fry the bacon until crispy, then remove with a slotted spoon and drain on kitchen paper.

Meanwhile, heat up the remaining oil in a smaller frying pan and crack in the eggs. Cook for approximately 1 minute, or until they are cooked to your liking. Add the vinegar to the bacon pan and heat for about 30 seconds, stirring well, then tip over the lettuce. Toss well, then top with the eggs and the bacon. Serve at once.

German Hot Potato with Bacon & Truffle Oil

Serves 6

1kg (2¼lb) potatoes (unpeeled weight), peeled

250g (9oz) smoked dry-cure back bacon, chopped

1 tablespoon olive oil

1 onion, peeled, chopped

1 medium free-range egg

75g (2¾oz) caster sugar

50ml (2floz) white wine vinegar

Salt and freshly ground black pepper

2 tablespoons freshly chopped flat-leaf parsley

Drizzle of truffle oil (optional)

The truffle oil used here is purely optional, as some people liken the aroma and taste of both black and white truffle oil to smelly socks rather than to one of the most alluring and evocative treats imaginable.

Cook the potatoes whole in boiling salted water until tender, then cool to barely warm. Cut into thick slices once cool enough to handle.

Fry the bacon in the olive oil in a heavy based frying pan until crispy, then remove with a slotted spoon and drain on kitchen paper. Add the onion and fry for about 10 minutes then remove, leaving the fat in the pan.

Beat together the egg, sugar and vinegar with 30ml (1floz) cold water, season with salt and pepper and add to the hot fat in the pan. Stirring constantly, bring slowly to the boil and cook over a medium heat for about 2 minutes until thickened. Return the bacon and onions to the pan and stir through.

Meanwhile, place the potatoes in a serving dish. Pour over the contents from the pan and add the chopped parsley. If using, drizzle with a tiny amount of truffle oil, and serve at once while still warm.

MACADAMIA, SMOKED CHICKEN & MINT SALAD

Serves 4

50g (1¾oz) macadamia nuts, partially crushed

2 large heads of chicory, separated, washed

110g (4oz) smoked chicken

3 tablespoons mint leaves

2 tablespoons sunflower oil

1 tablespoon nut oil (hazelnut, walnut or pistachio)

1 tablespoon raspberry vinegar

½ teaspoon Dijon mustard

Salt and freshly ground black pepper

Smoked turkey can be used instead of chicken if you prefer. And if you cannot find macadamia nuts – those wonderfully rich, buttery Australian nuts – then use blanched hazelnuts instead. To make this into a more substantial main course salad, add some crumbled feta cheese as you toss.

First toast the nuts: place the macadamia nuts on a sheet of baking foil and place under a preheated grill. Turning once, grill for 3–4 minutes, or until golden brown. Watch very carefully as they tend to burn quickly. Turn onto a board to cool.

Place the chicory leaves in a salad bowl, arranging them with the tips forming the outer rim. Cut the chicken into strips and roughly tear the mint leaves. Place these in the chicory-lined salad bowl together with the cooled nuts.

Whisk together the remaining ingredients and season with salt and pepper. Pour this all over the salad and toss just before serving.

A SALAD FOR ALL SEASONS

Perhaps because of the increasing numbers of 'ladies who lunch' and the wider appeal of healthy eating, main course salads are assuming a more prominent role in restaurants and at home. And whereas home salads used to consist of salad and cold meat made with yesterday's roast, they now use all sorts of ingredients from pheasant, fresh tuna or salt cod to goats' cheese or black pudding. New flavourings from abroad – North African, Far Eastern, Mexican – and, of course, the old favourites such as Italian, French, Chinese and Indian are becoming increasingly popular in salads.

There is a large range of interesting salad leaves and herbs now on offer: as well as sorrel, mint or round lettuce we now also have Japanese mizuna, Italian rucola and even Mexican cactus paddles. There is also a more exciting variety of breads available: once there was French stick (which was nothing like real French baguette) and that was it. Now we are rediscovering native breads and are proudly serving up loaves of soda or granary bread, tattie scones and stottie cake, while also taking more than just a passing glance at ciabatta, Lebanese flatbread and flour tortillas.

Allow your imagination to run riot with the endless possibilities of main course salads. Serve them after hot soup in winter or chilled soup in summer; follow with a hot steamed pudding in winter and a fresh fruit ice-cream or meringue in summer. Salads are versatile and variable, welcoming and easy.

CAESAR SALAD

Serves 2–3

1 cos lettuce, washed, torn or chopped into large pieces

2 thick slices of white bread, crusts removed, cubed

3 tablespoons olive oil, plus a little extra for frying

1 large free-range egg

1 large garlic clove, peeled, crushed

1 tablespoon lime juice

2 teaspoons Worcestershire sauce

4–5 anchovy fillets, chopped

Freshly ground black pepper

25g (1oz) Parmesan cheese, coarsely grated

According to Diana Kennedy in her seminal book, Mexican Regional Cooking, *the original Caesar Salad was made in Tijuana, Mexico by Caesar Cardini in 1926. First known as Aviator's Salad, because of the nearby air base in San Diego, it then became popularly known as Caesar's Salad.*

Place the cos in a salad bowl.

Fry the bread cubes in a little olive oil until crispy, then drain on kitchen paper.

Place the egg in a pan of cold water and bring to the boil. Boil for 1 minute then plunge into cold water to stop the cooking. Once it is cool enough to handle, crack the egg into a food processor and add the garlic, lime juice, Worcestershire sauce, anchovies and oil. Process well, then add pepper to taste (no salt is needed due to the saltiness of the anchovies).

To serve, pour the dressing over the leaves and add the croûtons and Parmesan. Toss well and serve at once.

AVOCADO CAESAR SALAD

Serves 2–3

The classic ingredients (see above)

2 avocados, peeled, diced

This is a variation on the classic Caesar Salad. If you wish, you can also add chunks of smoked chicken, cherry tomatoes and a handful of fresh herbs to provide even more oomph.

Make the salad as usual, and at the end toss in the avocado along with the Parmesan and croûtons.

CHEF SALAD

Serves 3–4

75 g (2¾ oz) salami, chopped

100 g (3½ oz) roast ham, chopped

2 hard-boiled free-range eggs, peeled, chopped

4–6 tomatoes, diced

¼ cucumber, diced

2–3 gherkins, chopped

75 g (2¾ oz) cheese, diced

6–8 crisp lettuce leaves, chopped

1 tablespoon mayonnaise (see page 154)

1 tablespoon olive oil

½ tablespoon lemon juice

½ teaspoon Dijon mustard

Salt and freshly ground black pepper

This is a simple salad which is full of all sorts of good things. It is very variable and you can add more or less anything interesting from your refrigerator or larder. For the cheese, use either an aged Gouda, Gruyère or Emmenthal. Cos is the best lettuce to use, but again, any crisp lettuce will do.

Combine the first eight ingredients together in a bowl.

Mix the mayonnaise, olive oil, lemon juice and mustard. Add a generous grinding of salt and pepper. Pour over the salad and toss before serving.

MUSHROOM SALAD WITH TRUFFLED FRIED EGG

Serves 2

3 tablespoons extra virgin olive oil

250 g (9 oz) large flat mushrooms, cut into 3–4 thick slices

The juice of ½ lemon

Salt and freshly ground black pepper

1 heaped tablespoon flat-leaf parsley

1 tablespoon truffle oil

2 large free-range eggs

A divine combination that is also wonderful eaten between two slabs of country bread. Both white and black truffle oil are good.

Heat the olive oil in a frying pan until very hot. Add the mushrooms and fry for about 10 minutes until tender and crispy on the edges, not slimy. Tip the mushrooms and oils from the pan into a bowl, add the lemon juice, salt and pepper. Leave to cool, then stir in the parsley. Do not chill.

Just before serving, heat the truffle oil in a frying pan and fry the eggs until just done – about 2 minutes. The yolks should still be runny. Tip the entire contents of the pan – oil and all – over the mushrooms and serve at once.

PAPAYA, PRAWN & STAR ANISE SALAD

Serves 4

600g (1 lb 5oz) large tiger prawns, cooked, shelled

2 large papayas, diced

6–8 spring onions, chopped

½ red chilli, finely chopped (or a dash or two of hot chilli sauce)

FOR THE DRESSING
6 star anise

Juice of 2 limes

1 tablespoon Thai fish sauce

1 tablespoon dark soy sauce

3 tablespoons sunflower oil

If you prefer to cook your own prawns, simply fry them in a spoonful or two of oil until done, then tip into the star anise dressing while warm. You can remove the star anise if you like, but I think they look attractive left in the salad. Just be sure to warn your guests that they are for decoration only and should not be eaten.

First, make the dressing. Place all the ingredients in a saucepan and heat gently without boiling until very warm, then remove from the heat, cover and leave to stand for about 1 hour, to allow the star anise flavour to develop.

Drain the prawns thoroughly if defrosted and pat dry. Place in a bowl with the papayas, spring onions and chilli. Once the dressing has cooled, pour it over the prawns and toss well together. Leave to stand for about 30 minutes, then serve at room temperature.

PRAWN, LIME & CORIANDER SALAD

Serves 4

750g (1lb 10oz) large king or tiger prawns, shelled, cleaned

2 tablespoons olive oil

The juice of 1 large lime

3 heaped tablespoons freshly chopped coriander

Salt and freshly ground black pepper

Lamb's lettuce or rocket, washed

For a light main course, allow 5–6 prawns per person. This salad also makes a good summer starter (allow 3–4 prawns per person). Serve with plenty of bread, preferably Middle Eastern flat bread. If you are using frozen prawns, be sure to defrost them and pat thoroughly dry before frying.

Gently pat the prawns dry if necessary, then heat the olive oil in a large heavy-based frying pan. As soon as it is hot, add the prawns and fry briskly for 2–3 minutes, turning them frequently, until the prawns are cooked to a healthy pink colour.

Once they are done, tip the entire contents of the pan into a bowl and add the lime juice, coriander and salt and pepper. Stir well, then allow to cool to room temperature or until barely warm.

Place a small amount of lamb's lettuce or rocket on each main plate, then top with some prawns and some of the juices. Serve at once.

CRAB SALAD WITH ORIENTAL VINAIGRETTE

Serves 4

450g (1lb) white crabmeat

1 tablespoon soy sauce

2 garlic cloves, peeled, finely chopped

The juice of 2 limes

1 heaped tablespoon freshly chopped mint

1 heaped tablespoon freshly chopped basil

2 heaped tablespoons freshly chopped coriander

1 red chilli, deseeded, finely chopped

1 tablespoon Thai fish sauce

1 tablespoon sunflower oil

Crisp salad leaves, preferably oriental

Coriander sprigs, to garnish

This is a lovely summery salad and is ideal for a buffet (ensuring it does not become too warm) or for a light supper, perhaps with some buttered new potatoes.

Place the crabmeat in a bowl (if frozen, ensure it is thoroughly thawed and dry).

Combine the next nine ingredients in another bowl and pour the dressing over the crab. Toss gently, then cover and refrigerate for a couple of hours. An hour or so before serving, arrange the salad leaves around a shallow serving dish. Heap the crab mixture into the middle and garnish with coriander sprigs.

SQUID WITH CHILLI DRESSING

Serves 3–4

1 tablespoon sunflower oil

1–3 red chillies, deseeded,
finely chopped

2 stalks of lemon grass, outer leaves
removed, inner part
finely chopped

2 fat garlic cloves, peeled,
finely chopped

1 young leek, washed,
finely chopped

4 spring onions, chopped

300g (10½oz) prepared squid, cut
into rings with tentacles left whole

1 tablespoon light soy sauce

1 tablespoon Thai fish sauce

2 heaped tablespoons freshly
chopped coriander

2 heaped tablespoons freshly
chopped mint

Salt and freshly ground
black pepper

Ask your fishmonger to clean the squid for you, but to leave you with the tentacles, which not only taste good but look wonderful, in a somewhat prehistoric way. Add as many chillies as you like – however I would not add more than three, for fear of overpowering the other flavours.

Heat the oil in a large frying pan or wok until hot, then add the chillies, lemon grass and garlic. Fry for about 30 seconds, then add the leek and spring onions and continue to cook for a further minute, still on a high heat. Add the squid and cook, stirring continuously, for 1–2 minutes until just done. (Do not overcook squid or it will become rubbery.) Add the soy and fish sauce, stir well and cook for 30 seconds, then remove and tip into a bowl and leave to cool.

When cool, stir in the coriander and mint, check the seasoning and serve at room temperature.

SCALLOPS WITH MACADAMIA MAYO

Serves 2

1 large egg yolk

½ teaspoon Dijon mustard

½ teaspoon lime juice

¼ teaspoon salt

75 ml (3 fl oz) sunflower oil

75 ml (3 fl oz) macadamia nut oil

Salt and freshly ground
black pepper

12 plump scallops

Olive oil, to fry

A generous handful of mizuna or
rocket

A handful of chopped roasted
macadamia nuts, to serve

This is based on a dish I ate in Tasmania, which was huge char-grilled prawns with macadamia nut mayonnaise. The oil used was an unfiltered one, chock-a-block with crushed macadamia nuts, and although this type of oil is not available in this country, the texture becomes similar if you scatter the dish with chopped roasted nuts just before serving.

First make the mayo: place the egg yolk in a small food processor (I use the mini bowl in my large food procesor; if you want, double the quantity and use a regular food processor). Whizz the yolk, mustard, lime juice and salt for a few seconds until mixed.

Pour the oils into a reliable jug then, very very slowly – drop by drop – pour in the oils. Only increase the flow from drop to thin stream once you see an emulsion has begun to form. Season to taste.

Ensure the scallops are clean and dry. Heat 1 tablespoon of olive oil in a heavy frying pan until very hot, then add the scallops and fry for about 1–2 minutes on each side, depending on thickness. Only turn them after 1 minute, to allow a crust to form.

To serve, place the mizuna or rocket in a bowl, top with the scallops, then dollop on some mayo. Scatter over some chopped nuts and serve at once, while the scallops are still warm.

SCALLOP, RICE NOODLE & CORIANDER SALAD

Serves 4

16–20 plump scallops, cleaned

250 g (9 oz) Thai rice noodles

5 tablespoons sunflower oil

4 spring onions, chopped

1 tablespoon sesame oil

1 tablespoon soy sauce

3 heaped tablespoons freshly chopped coriander

1 tablespoon rice vinegar

½–1 red chilli, finely chopped

Salt and freshly ground black pepper

The rice noodles should be served warm rather than hot and so should be cooked about 20 minutes before you are ready to start frying the scallops.

If the scallops have been in the refrigerator, be sure to bring them to room temperature for at least 30 minutes.

Cook the rice noodles according to the packet's instructions and drain well.

In a bowl, whisk together 4 tablespoons of sunflower oil with the remaining ingredients, then taste for seasoning. Pour this dressing over the noodles, stirring well.

Heat a heavy-based frying pan until hot, add the remaining sunflower oil and, once the oil is smoking hot, add half the scallops and fry for about 1 minute on each side until just cooked. Remove and fry the remaining scallops, with a little extra oil if necessary.

To serve, place a mound of noodles on a plate and top with 4–5 hot scallops. Eat at once.

SEAFOOD GUMBO SALAD

Serves 4

3 tablespoons olive oil

1 onion, peeled, chopped

2 fat garlic cloves, peeled, chopped

1 red pepper, deseeded, chopped

300g (10½oz) firm white fish, such as monkfish, cut into large chunks

200g (7oz) raw tiger or king prawns, shelled, deveined

200g (7oz) mussels, well scrubbed, debearded

300ml (10floz) hot fish stock

250g (9oz) okra, washed, trimmed

Salt and freshly ground black pepper

500g (1lb 2oz) cooked rice (this is the cooked weight)

2–3 tablespoons freshly chopped parsley

Tabasco (optional)

A gumbo is a one-dish meal that is part of the repertoire of the Cajun kitchen. Famous in Louisiana and in particular in New Orleans, gumbo can be made with chicken or a variety of seafood. I have used monkfish, prawns and mussels, but you could substitute oysters, crab or even lobster. One of the main ingredients is okra, also known as 'lady's fingers'. When cooked, the sticky juice that lies within the green pods lends a lovely, almost jelly-like finish to the stew and gives the characteristic silky smoothness of a gumbo.

To prepare okra, simply wash and dry them carefully, then cut off the stalks without cutting into the seed pods or they will lose their shape as they cook. Instead of being served hot with rice, this salad is mixed with cooked rice while hot and served at room temperature liberally sprinkled with parsley. A dash or two of Tabasco just before serving livens up the flavours beautifully.

Heat the oil in a large saucepan and fry the onion, garlic and pepper for about 10 minutes, or until softened.

Add the monkfish, prawns and mussels and stir gently. Cook over a high heat for 1 minute and stir to coat them in the oil. Then add the hot stock and the okra, with plenty of salt and pepper. Bring to the boil, then cover, reduce to a simmer and cook for about 10 minutes. Remove from the heat and tip everything into a bowl, with the rice, stirring well.

Allow to cool, then stir in the parsley and check the seasoning. Serve at room temperature with an optional dash of Tabasco.

LOBSTER, MANGO & PESTO SALAD

Serves 4

1 lobster, about 700–900g
(1 lb 9 oz–2 lb), freshly boiled

One crispy lettuce, washed

2 ripe mangoes, diced

4 tablespoons extra virgin olive oil

1 heaped tablespoon pesto
(see page 156)

1 tablespoon white wine vinegar

Salt and freshly ground
black pepper

Fresh basil leaves, to garnish

This recipe is for treats only due to the exorbitant price of lobsters. Since you need freshly cooked lobster, I would recommend you do the murderous deed yourself, unless you know your fishmonger well and he can cook it for you to order. All you need is a large pan – and a little Dutch courage if you are at all squeamish. Immerse the lobster in your pan of boiling water, return to a full boil and boil for 10 minutes per 450 g/1 lb. Then plunge directly into cold water to stop the cooking.

Remove the meat from the lobster body and claws and cut into large chunks. Place the lettuce in a shallow serving dish and top with the lobster meat and the mango. In a separate bowl, whisk together the oil, pesto and vinegar and season with salt and pepper. Pour this over the lobster and mango. Garnish with basil leaves. Serve at room temperature with plenty of sourdough bread.

CRISPY SALMON SKIN WITH PICKLED GINGER

Serves 2

A large piece of salmon skin
(from a fillet about 500 g/1 lb 2 oz
– you can use the actual flesh for
the following recipe)

1 heaped tablespoon Japanese
pickled ginger, chopped

1 crisp lettuce, washed

1 tablespoon hazelnut oil

½ tablespoon Japanese rice vinegar

Pinch of sugar

Salt and freshly ground
black pepper

I first tried grilled salmon skin in a sushi bar in Los Angeles. It was crispy, moist and delicious. Back home in Scotland, when chatting to my fishmonger, I discovered he has been grilling salmon skin on the barbecue for years. And who said the British were not an innovative people?

Preheat the grill. Place the skin on a piece of foil and cook under a hot grill for about 2 minutes on each side, or until crispy. Remove and snip into pieces when cool enough to handle.

Meanwhile, toss the pickled ginger with the lettuce in a bowl and add the oil, vinegar, sugar and some salt and pepper. Once tossed, scatter over the crispy skin and serve at once.

ROASTED SALMON WITH SMOKED SALMON DRESSING

Serves 4

4 medium-sized salmon fillets (about 200g/7oz), preferably middle-cut, skinned (see previous recipe)

Olive oil, for brushing

Salt and freshly ground black pepper

50g (1¾oz) tin of anchovies in oil

200ml (7floz) crème fraîche

200g (7oz) smoked salmon trimmings

3 tablespoons chives, chopped

The juice of 1 lemon

2 teaspoons horseradish sauce

1 large cos lettuce, washed

The dressing of this salad is unusual – a mixture of smoked salmon, anchovies and crème fraîche – but adds a lovely smokey, savoury tang to the quick-roasted salmon. It should be served warm as soon as the dressing has been poured. Top with crunchy croûtons to make it even more substantial.

Preheat the oven to 240°C/475°F/gas mark 9. Place the fillets on a roasting tray and brush lightly with olive oil. Season with salt and pepper, then roast in the oven for 7–8 minutes until just done (test with the tip of a sharp knife to see if the flesh is cooked). Remove from the oven and allow to rest for about 5 minutes.

Meanwhile, place the anchovies and their oil in a saucepan and slowly heat, stirring, until the anchovies break up. After a couple of minutes, add the crème fraîche and bring to the boil, again stirring. Simmer, uncovered, for about 5 minutes, then add the smoked salmon trimmings and chives and stir well. Simmer very gently for about 2 minutes, then remove from the heat, stir in the lemon juice and horseradish and add pepper to taste.

Place the salad leaves in a bowl and top with the roasted salmon. Pour the hot sauce over the top and serve at once.

PENNSYLVANIA DUTCH SAFFRON CHICKEN SALAD

Serves 6

1 free-range chicken, about 1.5–2 kg
(3 lb 5 oz–4 lb 8 oz), poached or
roasted, cut or torn into chunks

Cos lettuce, washed, roughly torn

FOR THE SAFFRON MAYONNAISE

Generous pinch of saffron threads

100 ml (3½ fl oz) sunflower oil

100 ml (3½ fl oz) olive oil

1 large egg yolk

1 teaspoon Dijon mustard

1 teaspoon lemon juice

Salt and freshly ground
black pepper

Chervil, chopped, to garnish

According to John Humphries' wonderful book, The Essential Saffron Companion, *amongst the earliest saffron users and cultivators in America were the Pennsylvania Dutch, a sect escaping religious persecution in the eighteenth century. Each year they staged a Midsummer fair which featured saffron bread and creamy chicken saffron pies. This salad is a combination of chicken and saffron, with the rich creamy mayonnaise replacing the creamy sauce of the chicken pies. For ideas on cooking the chicken, see page 70.*

First make the mayo. Soak the saffron in 1 tablespoon of boiling hot water for about 20 minutes. Mix the oils together and pour into a reliable jug. Place the egg yolk, mustard and half the lemon juice in a food processor, season well with salt and pepper and whizz for a few seconds until blended. Then, very slowly dribble in the oil with the machine running – literally drop by drop – until you can see an emulsion beginning to form. Then you can pour in a slow, thin, steady stream until all the oil has been amalgamated. Tip into a bowl and stir in the saffron liquid and the remaining lemon juice. Add extra salt and pepper if required. Chill for at least 12 hours, to allow the saffron flavour and colour to develop.

Arrange the cos lettuce on a shallow serving dish and season with salt and pepper. Tip the mayonnaise into a large bowl and add the chicken. Stir gently to coat, then pile this on top of the salad. Garnish with chervil and serve at room temperature.

CHICKEN SALAD WITH TUNA MAYO

Serves 8

1 large free-range chicken, about 2.25 kg (5 lb), poached or roasted

Cos, little gem or chicory, washed

400 g (14 oz) quality mayonnaise (see page 154)

400 g (14 oz) tin tuna, drained

50 g (1¾ oz) tin of anchovies, drained

50 ml (2 fl oz) dry vermouth

Salt and freshly ground black pepper

Capers or caper berries, to garnish

The idea for this recipe comes from two sources. One is that old buffet table favourite, coronation chicken – cold chicken swathed under a mantle (as they say in 'menu-speak') of curry mayonnaise. The other is the Italian 'vitello tonnato' – cold veal covered with tuna mayonnaise and topped with anchovies and capers. Both dishes are ideal for cold buffets, but this version – chicken in a tuna mayonnaise – is my favourite. You will need the meat from a large free-range chicken for this. Either poach in water with peppercorns, a bay leaf and a splash of wine, or roast with a smear of butter or drizzle of oil, basting frequently.

First remove the meat from the chicken and either slice neatly or roughly tear into chunks. Discard the skin and bones. Place the meat on a large platter lined with the salad leaves.

Place the mayonnaise, tuna, half the anchovies and the vermouth in a food processor and whizz until well combined. Taste and season accordingly.

Spoon the mayo over the chicken and garnish with the remaining anchovies and the capers or caper berries. Serve at room temperature.

CHICKEN SATAY SALAD

Serves 6

750g (1lb 10oz) free-range chicken fillets, skinned

2 tablespoons sunflower oil

1 tablespoon light soy sauce

The juice of 1 lime

15g (½oz) fresh coriander (stalks and leaves)

Crispy salad leaves

100g (3½oz) bean sprouts

FOR THE SAUCE

200g (7oz) sugar-free crunchy peanut butter

300ml (10fl oz) chicken stock

2 tablespoons dry sherry

1 tablespoon light soy sauce

The juice of 1 lime

2 teaspoons freshly grated ginger

1 tablespoon honey

2 garlic cloves, peeled, chopped

3 spring onions, chopped

1 teaspoon ground cumin

2 teaspoons chilli sauce

Salt and freshly ground black pepper

There are many variations of this popular Indonesian dish. Essentially it consists of pieces of meat which are marinated, then dried or barbecued and served with a spicy peanut sauce. Some recipes add Thai fish sauce, coconut or sesame oil, but mine, based on an Australian recipe given to me by my cousin after she spent a year in Queensland, uses crunchy peanut butter to give a lovely rough texture to the dipping sauce. When using wooden skewers or satay sticks, soak them first in water for at least 30 minutes to prevent burning.

Cut the chicken into small pieces (about 2.5cm/1in square). Combine the oil, soy sauce and lime juice in a bowl. Remove the stalks from the coriander leaves, chop and add to the bowl. Reserve the leaves for later. Add the chicken and coat with the sauce. Cover the bowl with clingfilm and refrigerate for 4–6 hours.

For the sauce, combine everything except the salt and pepper in a saucepan and bring very slowly to the bowl. Once the mixture begins to bubble, lower the heat, cover and cook for 10–15 minutes, stirring regularly, until thickened. Remove from the heat and cool for at least 5 minutes, then taste and check seasoning. If it seems too thick, stir in 1–2 tablespoons of boiling water.

Meanwhile, cook the chicken. Preheat the grill to high. Remove the meat from the marinade and thread 5–6 pieces of chicken onto each skewer, pushing the pieces close together. Place on a grill pan, brush lightly with oil and grill for 5–8 minutes, turning often, until done.

To serve, place some lettuce and bean sprouts in a shallow bowl. Top with the chicken satay (still on their sticks). Stir the chopped coriander leaves into the sauce and pour some of the sauce over the meat. Pour the rest into a bowl and serve alongside.

DUCK, PEA & GINGER SALAD

Serves 4

4 duck breasts, skin on

4 tablespoons olive oil

1 heaped tablespoon freshly
grated ginger

150g (5½oz) fresh or frozen peas

1 tablespoon red wine vinegar

Chicory or cos lettuce, washed

The flavour of ginger works beautifully with duck, as is often seen in Far Eastern recipes. And peas cooked with duck is a classic French dish. So, what better than a spot of 'fusion' cooking – duck salad with peas and ginger!

Preheat the oven to 220°C/425°F/gas mark 7. Heat a heavy-based frying pan until very hot. Using a sharp knife, score the skin of the duck breasts, then place them in the hot pan, skin-side down and without any added fat. Cook for 2 minutes, then turn and cook on the other side for 2 minutes. Transfer to a baking tray and cook in the oven for a further 12–15 minutes, depending on thickness, then remove and leave to rest for at least 10 minutes.

Heat the oil and the ginger together in a small saucepan and, when bubbles appear, cover with a lid and remove from the heat. Leave for about 20 minutes to infuse.

Cook the peas until just done, then refresh in cold water and dry well. Toss in the vinegar.

To assemble, pour the ginger oil and the peas (in vinegar) over the chicory or lettuce and toss well. Cut each duck breast into 5 or 6 slices and place on top of the salad. Serve at once garnished, if liked, with a mound of thinly sliced chicory.

DUCK WITH TAPENADE

Serves 2–3

2 large duck breasts

2 tablespoons tapenade
(see page 156)

2 tablespoons extra virgin olive oil

1 tablespoons balsamic vinegar

Freshly ground black pepper

1 cos lettuce, washed

6–8 large basil leaves

8–10 black olives, stoned

You can buy very good tapenade from most supermarkets or delicatessens, but I prefer to make my own if I have time. The recipe for tapenade and many other classic dressings can be found at the end of the book.

Preheat the oven to 220°C/425°F/gas mark 7. Score the skin of each breast. Heat a heavy-based frying pan until very hot, then place the duck breasts in, skin-side down (you do not need to add any oil). Cook for 2 minutes, then turn and cook for a further 1 minute. Transfer to a small roasting tin and roast in the oven for 12–15 minutes. Then remove and allow to rest for at least 15 minutes.

Whisk together the tapenade, oil and vinegar and season with pepper (no salt is required as the tapenade is salty).

Roughly tear the cos and basil leaves and place in a large salad bowl.

Cut each duck breast into 5 or 6 slices. Pour the dressing over the salad and toss well. Top with the duck and the black olives and serve at once.

COLD TURKEY WITH CRANBERRY VINAIGRETTE

Serves 6–8

50g (1¾oz) pecan nuts

Cos lettuce, or chicory leaves, washed and left whole

Leftover meat from 1 large turkey

2 heaped tablespoons cranberry sauce

3–4 tablespoons olive oil

1 tablespoon balsamic vinegar

Salt and freshly ground black pepper

Here is a festive salad that can make good use of leftover turkey and those dribs and drabs of cranberry sauce. If, however, you want to make this at a time when there is no fowl carcass lurking in your larder, then simply cook a whole turkey breast (poach or roast) until done, cool, then tear the meat into chunks.

Toast the pecan nuts. Preheat the grill. Place the nuts on a sheet of foil and grill for 2–3 minutes, turning once, until golden brown. The nuts can burn very easily so keep an eye on them.

Arrange the cos or chicory around a large platter. Chop the turkey meat into bite-sized chunks and place on top of the salad leaves.

Whisk together the cranberry sauce, oil and vinegar, and season well with salt and pepper. Spoon this all over the meat, then top with the toasted nuts.

ROAST CHICKEN WITH MANGO & LIME SALSA

Serves 4

2 large ripe mangoes, peeled, diced

4–6 spring onions, finely chopped

The juice of 2 limes

2 tablespoons fresh coriander, chopped

½–1 red chilli, finely chopped

Large bag of mixed salad leaves

300g (10½oz) cooked chicken, diced

2 tablespoons sunflower oil

Salt and freshly ground black pepper

If you have no leftover chicken, buy 2–3 chicken breasts and poach them until tender. Add extra chilli if you like it fiery.

For the salsa, place the mango, onions, lime juice, coriander and chilli in a bowl and combine gently, seasoning with salt and pepper to taste. Leave to stand for about an hour.

Place the salad leaves in a bowl, top with the chicken then drizzle over the oil. Top with the salsa and toss gently just before serving.

75

QUAIL WITH POMEGRANATE

Serves 2

4 oven-ready quails

1 teaspoon ground cumin

½ teaspoon ground coriander

½ teaspoon ground ginger

1 tablespoon lemon juice

2 tablespoons olive oil

1 round lettuce, washed

1 pomegranate

3 tablespoons extra virgin olive oil

1 tablespoon raspberry vinegar

Salt and freshly ground
black pepper

This dish looks stunning, with the bright pomegranate seeds sitting on top of spiced roast quails and a pile (or dare I say a nest) of fresh green lettuce. Serve this as a main course for two, or a starter for four.

Place the quails in a dish. Mix together the cumin, coriander, ginger, lemon juice and olive oil, then pour over the quails. Leave for about 1 hour in the refrigerator, spooning the marinade over from time to time.

Meanwhile, preheat the oven to 220°C/425°F/gas mark 7. Transfer the quails to a roasting tin and pour over the marinade. Roast for about 20 minutes, or until cooked. Allow them to cool for about 20 minutes.

Place the lettuce in a salad bowl. Cut the pomegranate in half over a bowl, to collect the juices. Scoop out the seeds and juices and mix together with the extra virgin oil, vinegar and salt and pepper.

To serve, place the quail on top of the lettuce, spoon over a little of the pan juices, then top with the pomegranate dressing. Toss gently and serve at once.

PHEASANT WITH MANGO

Serves 3–4

1 young plump pheasant,
oven-ready

Salt and freshly ground
black pepper

25g (1oz) unsalted butter, softened

1 large ripe mango, peeled, diced,
plus slices to garnish (optional)

2 tablespoons mango pickle

200ml (7fl oz) crème fraîche

The juice of 1 lemon

3–4 sticks celery, chopped (keeping
the leaves whole as garnish)

2 large heads of chicory, leaves
separated

This is a lovely combination of succulent roast pheasant topped with a creamy, tangy mango sauce. Try to cook the pheasant shortly before serving, as the dish is better when the meat is still slightly warm. It is important that you use a traditional Indian pickle (not a sweet chutney) as the pickle is far spicier. Stir the pickle before using, as the oil usually accumulates at the top of the jar leaving the good stuff at the bottom.

First roast the pheasant. Preheat the oven to 220°C/425°F/gas mark 7. Season the pheasant with salt and pepper, then smear the butter all over the top. Place in a small roasting tin and roast for 30 minutes, basting once, then remove and cool in the tin for at least 30 minutes.

Meanwhile, place the half the mango in a food processor with the pickle, crème fraîche and lemon juice. Whizz until well combined, then check the seasoning – you probably won't need anything if the pickle is as fiery as mine. This mixture can now be covered and chilled until needed so long as you bring it to room termperature before serving.

To serve, place the celery and chicory in a bowl with the remaining diced mango. Season the leaves. Carve the pheasant, removing as much meat as possible. Place this on top of the celery and chicory and garnish the dish with celery leaves. Spoon over some of the mango sauce and pour the rest into a small bowl, to offer as extras at the table. Garnish with slices of fresh mango, if desired.

SALMAGUNDI

Serves 4–6

1 cos lettuce, washed, chopped

Cold chicken or turkey, chopped

A handful of anchovy fillets, chopped

Cold ham, pork or beef, chopped

A handful of seeded grapes, halved

A handful of raisins

A handful of shelled walnuts

3–4 hard-boiled free-range eggs, quartered

5–6 spring onions, chopped

Cooked French beans

Large handfuls of fresh herb leaves

A handful of edible flowers

1 large unwaxed lemon, scrubbed, very thinly sliced, chopped

FOR THE DRESSING

1 tablespoon lemon juice

½ teaspoon Dijon mustard

4 tablespoons extra virgin olive oil

Salt and freshly ground black pepper

This Tudor salad, which is also called Solomongundi, Salamongundy and Sallid Magundi, is a general mish-mash of every sort of ingredient you can think of, served with a lemony dressing. In Hannah Glasse's cookbook of 1747, her ingredients included minced fowl, pickled herring, pickled red cabbage, cold pigeon, parsley, hard-boiled eggs, pickles, sliced lemons and 'station flowers', which I take to mean marigolds and pansies. For my recipe, you can obviously substitute any number of ingredients, but do keep in the thinly sliced lemon, some sort of cold meats, hard-boiled eggs and as many fresh herbs as you can lay your hands on. I have not given precise quantities as you can simply make as large a bowl of this salad as you wish. Incidentally, in case you thought the craze for good olive oil was relatively recent, there is reference in John Evelyn's Acetaria, A Discourse of Sallets, *written in 1699, of good olive oil. He recommends dressing salads in a smooth, light oil that is 'pleasant to the tongue', such as an oil made from native Lucca olives. So perhaps there was life before salad cream after all.*

The best way to serve this is to arrange the lettuce in the base of a large, shallow serving dish. Top with all the other ingredients, which should be chopped to roughly the same size. Whisk together the dressing ingredients with salt and pepper, then drizzle over the salad, toss and serve.

WARM BIRYANI SALAD

Serves 6

2 tablespoons sunflower oil

1 onion, peeled, finely chopped

6 cardamom pods

2.5 cm (1 in) cinnamon stick

2 cloves

Tiny pinch of saffron

300 g (10½ oz) boned leg of lamb, cut into thin chunks

350 g (12 oz) basmati rice

Approximately 900 ml (30 fl oz) hot lamb stock

Salt and freshly ground black pepper

3 tablespoons natural yoghurt

The juice of 1 large lime

4 tablespoons freshly chopped mint leaves

This is a warm salad, based on that splendid festive Mughlai dish, lamb biryani. One of the finest biryanis I have tasted was in Delhi where chef Gev Desai prepared a dish delicately flavoured with exotic and fragrant spices and bolstered with the most delicious buttery basmati rice. His secret ingredient was a tiny phial of what looked and smelt like perfume, but which was in fact an exotic flower water. The flavour of the entire dish was enhanced greatly by only a couple of drops. Serve this dish warm, not hot or cold, and accompany it with the traditional side dishes of hard-boiled eggs, fried onions, sultanas and whole blanched almonds.

Heat the oil in a saucepan and gently fry the onion until softened. Add the cardamom, cinnamon, cloves and saffron and fry briskly for 1 minute, until they crackle. Stir well. Add the lamb and brown all over, on a high heat, then remove the lamb with a slotted spoon. Reduce the heat to medium, add the rice, stir well until coated, then add the hot stock.

Bring slowly to the boil and stir. Return the meat to the pan, lower to a simmer, cover and cook for about 15–20 minutes, until the rice is done. You may need extra stock. Season generously with salt and pepper. Leave for at least 10 minutes until warm, not hot.

Mix together the yoghurt, lime juice and mint and add to the pan, stirring well to combine. Check the seasoning again and serve warm.

INDONESIAN PEANUT SALAD WITH STIR-FRIED PORK

Serves 4

2 teaspoons soy sauce

2 tablespoons sunflower oil

450g (1lb) pork fillet, cut into strips

50g (1¾oz) unsalted peanuts

1 heaped tablespoon crunchy
no-sugar peanut butter

The juice of 1 lemon

1 tablespoon Thai fish sauce

3 tablespoons fresh coriander, plus
extra to garnish

4 spring onions, chopped

1 teaspoon molasses sugar

Salt and freshly ground
black pepper

250g (9oz) oriental noodles

100g (3½oz) bean sprouts

*This is a combination of two mainstream Indonesian recipes –
satay and gado-gado, a fabulous salad with a huge variety of
ingredients (not unlike the old English 'salmagundi', see page 80)
and with different flavours and textures. It usually includes
cabbage, bean sprouts, carrots, celery and hard-boiled eggs, all
dressed in a peanut and coconut sauce. I have omitted the
coconut from this dressing and added plenty of fresh coriander
for extra colour and flavour. You can also add a little grated
ginger if you wish.*

Heat the soy sauce and half the oil in a large frying pan.
Add the pork and stir-fry over a high heat for a few
minutes until cooked through and golden brown. Remove
and drain on kitchen paper.

Meanwhile, place the peanuts, peanut butter, lemon juice,
fish sauce, coriander, onions and sugar in a food processor
and blend until well mixed. Season to taste with salt and
freshly ground pepper.

Boil the noodles as instructed on the packet, then drain
and toss in the remaining oil. Stir in the bean sprouts.

To serve, place the noodles and sprouts on a large shallow
serving dish. Top with the pork. Spoon over the sauce and
garnish with some coriander leaves. Serve barely warm.

Pasta, Sausage & Fried Aubergine Salad

Serves 4–6

500 g (1 lb 2 oz) penne pasta

500 g (1 lb 2 oz) coarse pork sausages (or sausage of your choice)

1 large aubergine, wiped, cut into large dice

6 tablespoons olive oil

2 heaped tablespoons basil leaves

1 tablespoon sherry vinegar

1 heaped teaspoon Dijon mustard

Salt and freshly ground black pepper

Basil sprigs, to serve

Use your favourite sausages for this – classic coarse pork, herby pork or beef sausages are all good. Leftovers of this dish can be tipped into an ovenproof dish and sprinkled with Mozzarella, then drizzled with a spoonful of olive oil, covered loosely with foil and baked in a medium oven for 30 minutes or so until hot.

Cook the pasta according to the packet's instructions, then drain and keep warm. Meanwhile, grill the sausages until cooked, then cut into large chunks. Fry the aubergine in about 2 tablespoons of oil until tender and golden brown.

Mix together the remaining oil with the basil, vinegar and mustard and season with salt and pepper. While everything is still warm, toss the pasta, sausage and aubergine chunks together with the dressing, adding a little more oil if you think it needs it. Cool to room temperature before serving, garnished with sprigs of basil.

WARM BLACK PUDDING & SESAME SALAD

Serves 4

Large bag of mixed salad leaves

Salt and freshly ground
black pepper

1 tablespoon sesame oil

2 tablespoons olive oil

2 thick slices of white bread, crusts
removed, cubed

200g (7oz) black pudding, skin
removed, cut into bite-sized chunks

1 heaped tablespoon sesame seeds

1 tablespoon red wine vinegar

I realise black pudding is not everyone's cup of tea, but, presuming you have top-quality black pudding from a reliable butcher, it can be a wonderful and memorable treat. Depending on where you live, it will be made differently. Traditionally it is made from pig's blood mixed with fats, cereals and spices. It is often made with ox blood these days. In the western isles of Scotland, it is made from sheep's blood and mixed with plenty of oatmeal to give a texture not unlike a good haggis and a taste reminiscent of mutton. I have never been able to face sliced black pudding for breakfast, but served like this – cut into chunks, then quickly fried until crunchy outside and meltingly soft inside – it is divine.

Place the salad leaves in a bowl, season well, then toss in the sesame oil.

Heat the olive oil in a frying pan and fry the bread for 2–3 minutes until crispy. Drain on kitchen paper, then fry the black pudding (adding extra olive oil if necessary) over a high heat for 3–4 minutes, or until crunchy outside and hot inside. Add the sesame seeds, stir for a few seconds, then add the vinegar to the frying pan. Remove from the heat and tip everything over the salad, with the croûtons. Serve at once.

THAI BEEF & CHILLI SALAD

Serves 4

500g (1lb 2oz) piece of beef fillet tail

1 tablespoon light soy sauce

1 teaspoon sugar

4 teaspoons Thai fish sauce

6 tablespoons sunflower oil

Salt and freshly ground black pepper

2 heaped tablespoons coriander leaves

1 red chilli (try Thai or bird pepper for extra heat), deseeded, chopped

1 plump stalk of lemon grass, outer leaves removed and inner stalk chopped

4 spring onions, chopped

The juice of 1 lime

2 generous handfuls of mizuna, rocket or watercress

The flavours of this dish are fresh and punchy, depending on your chilli tolerance – you can always add an extra one for luck. Remember to allow an hour before cooking begins, for the marinating; and be sure to rest the meat well before slicing, to allow the juices to relax.

Place the beef in a small dish. Mix together the soy sauce, sugar, half the fish sauce and 1 tablespoon oil, then pour this over the meat, coating it well. Season with plenty of ground pepper and leave to marinate for 1 hour.

Now make the dressing: place the coriander, most of the chilli, lemon grass, spring onion and lime juice in a food processor and add the remaining fish sauce and oil. Process until thoroughly combined, then add salt and pepper to taste.

Preheat the oven to 220°C/425°F/gas mark 7. Place the beef in a small roasting tin, pour the soy sauce marinade over, and roast for 25 minutes, then remove and rest for at least 10 minutes.

Pile the salad leaves into a shallow serving dish and season. Slice the beef into thin slices and place on top. Spoon over the dressing, garnish with any remaining chilli, and serve at once.

CARPETBAG SALAD WITH HORSERADISH

Serves 4

3 large or 4 medium sirloin steaks

2 tablespoons oyster sauce

1 red pepper

Mixed salad leaves (rocket, lollo rosso, watercress)

4 tablespoons olive oil

2 teaspoons horseradish sauce

1 tablespoon raspberry vinegar

Salt and freshly ground black pepper

1 tablespoon sunflower or groundnut oil

4 shucked oysters (optional)

Carpetbag steak – a thick steak stuffed with oysters – is perhaps not something many of us would eat on a daily basis. Apart from the price, this is a hearty dish that would leave little room for any accompaniments such as potatoes or vegetables, never mind a yummy pudding to follow. My carpetbag salad is quite simply a steak marinated in Chinese oyster sauce, then fried and served on a horseradish-dressed salad. If you feel like gilding the lily, then shuck four oysters and place them on top of the steak just before serving; be sure to pour over the precious juice from the shells too.

Marinate the steaks in the oyster sauce for about 1 hour.

Preheat the grill. When hot, grill the pepper whole until the skin is charred, then wrap in foil. After about 20 minutes, slip off the skin, then slice the flesh into slivers.

Place the salad in a bowl. Put the olive oil, horseradish sauce and vinegar in a screw-top jar, shake to mix and season with salt and pepper to taste.

Heat a frying pan until very hot, then add the sunflower or groundnut oil. Place the steaks (and their oyster sauce coating) in the pan and fry for about 5 minutes, turning once, until medium-rare.

To serve, toss the dressing over the salad and top with the peppers. Slice the steaks into thick slices and place on top of the salad. If you are using fresh oysters, place them on top now. Serve at once.

A BIT ON THE SIDE

The words 'side salad' used to send shivers down my spine. I knew what to expect and if it contained anything more exciting than a leaf of lettuce, some tomato and a slice of cucumber, there would be whoops of joy from all around. But now, a salad to accompany a main course can be a thing of great beauty, a cornucopia of exotic and unusual ingredients, a melting pot of produce from all parts of the globe.

On my travels, I always find it interesting to see what locals do with their indigenous and locally grown salad ingredients and how they present and dress them. Some of these examples are to be found in this chapter. The Finnish potato salad was one that I enjoyed often during the year I spent in Lapland. Turkish aubergine and mint yoghurt salad was a favourite on the Turkish 'mezze' table during family summer holidays. Elephant foot bread with avocado was a delicious combination I ate while on safari in South Africa – and with a name like that, how could you not want to taste, enjoy, then demand the recipe?

Although salads should usually be tossed at the last minute to ensure crisp, fresh leaves, many of these salads – particularly the more substantial – are designed for buffet tables and large parties and so can be fully prepared in advance. Indeed some are better when the dressing has had time to soak in and the flavours have fully developed. Whichever salad you choose, and whether it is to be tossed and served at once or made well in advance, think fresh – and you cannot possibly go wrong.

ROASTED BUTTERNUT SQUASH SALAD

Serves 4

1 large butternut squash, about
1 kg (2 lb 4 oz), unpeeled weight

2 tablespoons olive oil

2 tomatoes, diced

½ red onion, peeled, finely chopped

1 tablespoon sesame oil

2 tablespoons sunflower oil

The juice of 1 lime

2 tablespoons freshly chopped
coriander

Salt and freshly ground
black pepper

This brightly coloured salad also works with pumpkin when it is in season. You will need about half a smallish pumpkin. Do not discard the pumpkin or squash seeds, but convert them into crunchy nibbles to accompany drinks. Rinse them thoroughly, dry, then place on a roasting tray with a drizzle of olive oil. Place in a medium-hot oven for about 25 minutes (checking that they do not burn), sprinkle with salt and serve.

Preheat the oven to 200°C/400°F/gas mark 6. Peel the squash and remove any fibrous pieces and the seeds. Cut into large (but mouth-sized) chunks. Place in a roasting tin with the olive oil and roast in the oven for about 30–35 minutes until tender but not too soft. Remove and allow to cool in the tin.

When cool, tip the squash into a large bowl with all the remaining ingredients and season to taste with salt and pepper. Serve at room temperature.

GRILLED FIG & PARMESAN SALAD

Serves 4–6

4 fresh figs, quartered

1 small cos lettuce, washed

2 small heads of chicory

3 tablespoons olive oil

1 tablespoon balsamic vinegar

2–3 sprigs of fresh thyme

Salt and freshly ground
black pepper

25 g (1 oz) Parmesan cheese
shavings ('shaved' from a block with
a vegetable peeler)

This is a wonderful way to use fresh figs during their short season. Once grilled, they are served hot with salad leaves and Parmesan. Snippets of Parma ham make it more substantial.

Preheat the grill. Place the figs on a grill tray and place under the grill for 2–3 minutes, or until just beginning to take on colour.

Meanwhile, place the lettuce and chicory (torn if necessary) in a large salad bowl. Mix together the oil, vinegar and thyme with some salt and pepper. Pour over the salad and toss through.

Once the figs are done, place them on top of the lettuce, then top with the Parmesan shavings. Eat at once.

LEBANESE SALAD WITH TAHINI DRESSING

Serves 4–6

1 large crispy lettuce, washed

A bag of purslane or lamb's lettuce, washed

½ cucumber, wiped, cut into slivers

3–4 spring onions, chopped

3 large tomatoes, chopped

FOR THE DRESSING

1 tablespoon tahini (be sure to stir well before spooning from the jar)

The juice of 2 lemons

1 tablespoon freshly chopped flat-leaf parsley

1 tablespoon freshly chopped mint

2 garlic cloves, peeled, crushed

1 tablespoon olive oil

Salt (optional) and freshly ground black pepper

I well remember my first Lebanese meal, where the first course was simply called 'Lebanese salad'. It was like a do-it-yourself, Blue Peter assembly kit for one of those designer salads we all know so well these days. It was literally a whole (admittedly smallish) cucumber, a pile of crisp lettuce leaves and some bright red tomatoes on a platter with appropriate cutting implements, a lemon and a canister of olive oil. As this was quite a smart restaurant, I was a little surprised to say the least. But it was certainly a talking point and, I have to say, the salad tasted excellent, once we had chopped it up ourselves. This recipe is for a salad which you can prepare before setting it on the table. It is then tossed in a dressing flavoured with lots of lemon juice and tahini, that sesame paste or pulp which is ubiquitous throughout Lebanon, Greece and Turkey.

Place the first five ingredients in a large bowl. For the dressing, whisk together the remaining ingredients and taste for seasoning – you will probably require only pepper. Toss the salad in the dressing and serve at once.

CACIK

Serves 6

1 cucumber

500g (1lb 2oz) Greek yoghurt

2 large garlic cloves, peeled, chopped

15g (½oz) freshly chopped dill

Salt and freshly ground black pepper

A Turkish recipe, this cucumber and yoghurt dish is ideal to have around at a barbecue. It goes well with all sorts of seafood and also with lamb, beef or vegetables. Be sure to drain the cucumber thoroughly to prevent the dish becoming watery.

Grate the cucumber (I do this in my food processor). Place the grated cucumber in a large sieve and press down with the back of a spoon to eliminate the liquid. Leave for an hour or so, then press again.

Mix the well-drained cucumber with the yoghurt, garlic and dill, then season with salt and pepper. You will need about 2 teaspoons of salt. Leave somewhere cool for at least an hour to allow the flavours to develop.

RED RICE & BASIL SALAD

Serves 6

375g (13oz) Camargue red rice

4 tablespoons olive oil (preferably a Provençal oil)

A large handful of fresh basil (preferably red or opal basil)

Salt and freshly ground black pepper

In the olden days there was rice, plain and simple. Now we have different shapes and sizes and, interestingly, colours. Camargue red rice has a lovely warm colour and a good nutty flavour. It can be served freshly cooked and warm, or cold in a salad (see right).

Bring a large saucepan of salted water to the boil. Add the rice and cook for about 35–40 minutes, or until cooked. (It is impossible to overcook red rice, which is a huge advantage!)

Drain well, then, while still warm, add the oil, stir and allow to cool. Tear the basil and mix with the rice, season to taste and serve at room temperature.

Spicy Daikon Salad with Wasabi Dressing

Serves 4

600g (1 lb 5oz) daikon (about 2 daikons)

2 tablespoons rice or cider vinegar

Salt and freshly ground black pepper

3 tablespoons sunflower oil

1 tablespoon mustard seeds

1–2 teaspoons wasabi

2 tablespoons freshly chopped coriander

Also known as mooli and white radish, daikon is now widely available in Asian stores and some Chinese supermarkets. Unlike our own smaller red radish, daikon can also be cooked. Boil or steam it until tender, then serve with a punchy oriental-style dressing, such as the one given here for this raw daikon salad. Wasabi is a Japanese condiment available either in its powdered form or as a paste in tubes. It is extremely sharp and highly recommended for unblocking the sinuses!

Coarsely grate the daikon, then squeeze gently in your hands to eliminate any excess liquid. Place in a bowl and stir in the vinegar and plenty of salt and pepper.

Heat the oil in a pan and fry the mustard seeds over a medium heat for 3–4 minutes or until they begin to pop. Remove from the heat, stir in the wasabi (taste and decide for yourself how much of a kick you want) and pour over the daikon. Stir in the coriander, taste again and serve at room temperature.

Couscous & Grilled Pepper Salad

Serves 6

200 g (7 oz) couscous

300 ml (10 fl oz) boiling water

3 peppers, preferably 1 red,
1 orange, 1 yellow (do not
use green)

½ teaspoon salt

4 tablespoons olive oil

1 tablespoon white wine vinegar

2 garlic cloves, peeled, crushed

Freshly ground black pepper

2 tablespoons freshly chopped
oregano

Couscous is wonderfully versatile. You can serve it hot, with a drizzle of olive oil or melted butter and plenty of freshly chopped herbs such as mint, parsley, coriander or oregano. A squeeze of lemon or some grated orange zest makes it even more delicious, and it tastes just as good served cold. This salad is dotted with diced grilled pepper and flavoured with oregano. It is a good accompaniment to baked or barbecued salmon or roast lamb. Add some cubes of feta cheese and you have a vegetarian main course. Most couscous available nowadays is pre-cooked, so all you have to do is soak it in boiling water or stock.

Place the couscous in a wide, shallow bowl and cover with the water. Fork through, then cover tightly with a doubled tea-towel. Leave to stand for about 20 minutes.

Meanwhile, preheat the grill. Quarter the peppers and remove the seeds and membrane. Place on a sheet of foil on a grill tray and grill for about 5–10 minutes until charred and blistered. Remove from the grill and wrap tightly in the foil. Leave for about 15 minutes to loosen the skin. Then remove the skin and wipe with kitchen paper, and cut into dice.

Fork through the couscous to remove any lumps. Add the salt. Whisk together the oil, vinegar, garlic, salt and pepper and pour over the couscous. Stir well, then allow to cool.

Once cool, add the peppers and oregano and stir. Check seasoning and serve at room temperature.

Mizuna & Tomato Salad

Serves 4–6

150–175g (5½–6 oz) mizuna, prepared

4–5 plum tomatoes, sliced

5 tablespoons olive oil

1 tablespoon sherry vinegar

2 garlic cloves, peeled, crushed

Salt and freshly ground black pepper

Mizuna, a Japanese salad leaf, has a nice peppery taste and an attractive frilly leaf that makes it a welcome addition to many mixed green salads (see left).

Place the mizuna in a shallow salad bowl and arrange the tomato slices on top.

In a screw-top jar, shake together the oil, vinegar, garlic and lots of salt and pepper. Just before serving, pour over the salad and eat with plenty of warm bread.

Tomato, Caper & Oregano Salad

Serves 4–6

3 large tomatoes (at room temperature), sliced

2–3 tablespoons capers, drained

1 heaped tablespoon fresh oregano, torn

2–3 tablespoons extra virgin olive oil

Salt and freshly ground black pepper

If you cannot find fresh oregano use marjoram instead. Do not resort to dried.

Arrange the tomatoes on a shallow serving dish, top with the capers then strew over the oregano. Drizzle with the oil, season with salt and pepper and eat at once.

FINNISH POTATO WITH SOUR CREAM & DILL

Serves 4

700g (1lb 9oz) tiny new potatoes,
well-scrubbed

2 gherkins, chopped

1 small leek, cleaned, finely
chopped

1 crisp eating apple, unpeeled,
chopped

150ml (5floz) smetana or
sour cream

2 tablespoons mayonnaise
(see page 154)

1 teaspoon Dijon mustard

2 tablespoons freshly chopped dill

1 teaspoon white wine vinegar

Salt and freshly ground
black pepper

Finland was the first country where I ever tasted potatoes with dill. After my time living there, I came across them in Sweden, Denmark and also Russia, but it was the simplicity of the Finnish combination that stuck with me. Sometimes they are simply boiled with dill fronds in the pan and sometimes they are tossed in butter flavoured with plenty of chopped fresh dill. Although Finland is such a cold country with an uncompromising climate of freezing winters with deep snow that lies from October until May, I tasted some of the freshest foods I had ever eaten. Tiny woodland berries provided much of the Finns' essential vitamin C in the northerly town where I lived. And to supplement the meat (mainly reindeer) and fish (mainly freshwater lake fish) were plenty of lovely salads, often spiked with fresh dill. This salad is one that was frequently served with rings of smoked sausages which the Finns eat with relish. They love to split them open and tuck in a squoosh of mustard and some cheese, then wrap them in foil and warm in the oven, over a bonfire or even over the sauna stones. If you cannot find smetana, sour cream will do.

Boil the potatoes until tender, then drain well and cool until barely warm. Mix together the remaining ingredients and season well with salt and pepper. Pour over the lukewarm potatoes and stir very gently to coat. Serve at room temperature.

MUSHROOM & SOUR CREAM SALAD

Serves 4

500g (1lb 2oz) large mushrooms, thickly sliced

The juice of 1 lemon

150ml (5fl oz) sour cream

½ red onion, peeled, finely chopped

Pinch of sugar

2 teaspoons salt

Freshly ground black pepper

Based on another Finnish recipe called 'Sienisalaatti', this is just the type of salad I often ate during my time spent in the frozen north. The Finns use wild mushrooms gathered in the woods, but out of season they would use button mushrooms or their own home-pickled mushrooms. I have substituted sour cream for the typically eastern smetana, but use this if you can find it.

Place the mushroom in a large pan with 500ml (18fl oz) water and lemon juice. Bring to the boil, then boil for 1 minute. Remove at once and drain. Pat the mushrooms thoroughly dry with kitchen paper.

Once they are completely dry, tip into a bowl and combine thoroughly with the remaining ingredients, adding plenty of ground pepper to taste. Serve at room temperature.

BRUSSELS SPROUT COLESLAW

Serves 6

500g (1lb 2oz) Brussels sprouts, trimmed, shredded

200g (7oz) carrots, peeled, grated

4 spring onions, chopped

3 tablespoons mayonnaise (see page 154)

1 tablespoon fromage frais

1 tablespoon lemon juice

1 teaspoon Dijon mustard

Salt and freshly ground black pepper

This is a wonderful dish to make during the winter months when there is a plethora of sprouts in the shops, but only so many festive turkeys to serve them with. This coleslaw can be served with baked potatoes, sandwiches or cold pork pies.

Place the prepared vegetables in a bowl. In a smaller bowl mix together the remaining ingredients and season well with salt and pepper. Tip the dressing over the vegetables and toss well to coat. Serve at room temperature, not straight from the refrigerator.

Barley & Porcini Salad

Serves 6

40g (1½oz) dried porcini

200ml (7fl oz) dry white wine

6 tablespoons olive oil

2 garlic cloves, peeled, chopped

1 red onion, peeled, chopped

3 sticks of celery, chopped

500g (1lb 2oz) pearl barley

550ml (19fl oz) hot chicken stock

Salt and freshly ground
black pepper

3 tablespoons freshly chopped
flat-leaf parsley

1 tablespoon sherry vinegar

A packet of dried porcini (ceps) is a larder essential. A quick rinse and a soak for half an hour and you have the makings of a superb dish. They can be added to pasta, rice, meat or grains. Indeed, they add texture and flavour to any dish. Try this unusual barley salad which is good served with roasts, barbecues or grills.

Rinse the mushrooms, then soak in the dry white wine for at least 30 minutes.

Preheat the oven to 170°C/325°F/gas mark 3. Heat half the oil in a heavy, ovenproof pan and gently fry the garlic, onion and celery for about 10 minutes, then add the barley. Stir well and cook for about 1 minute, then add the soaked porcini and their liquor. Add the hot stock and stir. Bring to the boil, season generously with salt and pepper and cover. Transfer to the oven for 30 minutes. Remove, fluff up with a fork and allow to cool.

Stir in the parsley and the remaining oil and the vinegar. Check the seasoning and serve at room temperature.

ROASTED TOMATO SALAD

Serves 4

8 large plum tomatoes, halved

Salt and freshly ground
black pepper

½ teaspoon sugar

3 tablespoons olive oil

2 garlic cloves, peeled, chopped

3 fat sprigs of fresh oregano

1 tablespoon chopped anchovies

1 tablespoon chopped green olives,
stoned

1 teaspoon capers

1 tablespoon balsamic vinegar

Like everything else, you get out of cooking what you put in. And with some ingredients you can fiddle around so that a slightly inferior product comes out as rather good or even excellent. Stale bread can be revitalized by frying up as croûtons or converting into an exotic Middle-Eastern salad by soaking it in lemon juice and oil and tossing with loads of fresh herbs and chopped salad. Squashed fruit can be converted into pies or crumbles; plain, dull-looking olives from a tin can be marinated in good olive oil and zapped with some chopped fresh chilli and a sprig or two of herbs. But when it comes to tomatoes, there is not much you can do with an inferior one. Of course you can sling them into sauces, soups and stews, but they will still require quite a lot of seasoning and usually some sugar to bring out any flavour they might have. For most of the year, I buy only southern tomatoes that have actually seen the sun as this is what gives them their sweetness. But British tomatoes are now coming on in leaps and bounds and those left to ripen on the vine vie with imported southern tomatoes. Our own baby plum and Flavia varieties are particularly tasty. This recipe brings out the best in any tomato – but of course tastes best of all with sun-ripened ones which have that perfect balance of sweet and acid.

Preheat the oven to 220°C/425°F/gas mark 7. Place the tomatoes on a baking sheet, cut side up. Sprinkle with salt, pepper and sugar and drizzle the oil over. Roast for 30 minutes, then reduce the oven to 150°C/300°F/gas mark 2. Scatter the garlic and two sprigs of oregano over the tomatoes and return to the oven for about 1–1½ hours or until the tomatoes are tinged a golden brown.

Place carefully, with all their juices, on a shallow serving dish and top with the anchovies, olives and capers. Drizzle over the balsamic vinegar and garnish with the remaining oregano leaves. Serve at room temperature.

SPINACH & NUTMEG SALAD

Serves 4

125g (4½oz) young spinach, washed

Salt and freshly ground black pepper

2 tablespoons olive oil

1 tablespoon walnut or hazelnut oil

One whole nutmeg

½ tablespoon cider vinegar

During a stay in Grenada, on the trail of nutmeg and mace, I came across many ways the locals use nutmeg, apart from in their famous and extremely potent rum punch. A local green vegetable called 'callaloo' – vaguely like spinach – is often cooked with nutmeg in soups and stews and as a vegetable. In this salad, young spinach is tossed in a light nutmeg dressing, to emulate the nutmeg vinaigrettes I enjoyed on that beautiful Caribbean island. Add some grated onion if you want a little more edge to this recipe.

Place the spinach in a salad bowl and season well with salt and pepper.

Place the oils in a small saucepan and grate in about ¼ teaspoon of nutmeg. It is important to use freshly grated nutmeg; do not use ready-grated. Heat over a low heat for a couple of minutes until it is barely hot, then remove and cover. Leave for about 20 minutes to infuse, then toss over the spinach with the vinegar. Mix well and serve at once.

PASTA, ASPARAGUS & PECORINO SALAD

Serves 4–6

300g (10½oz) tagliatelle

3–4 tablespoons olive oil

250g (9oz) asparagus, halved

125g (4½oz) Pecorino cheese

1 heaped tablespoon pesto
(see page 156)

Salt and freshly ground
black pepper

Fresh basil, to garnish

During those few weeks when local asparagus is in season, you should try this salad. It is essential to use real Pecorino cheese (made from unpasteurised ewes' milk in Sardinia) for its full, rather salty flavour. Since Parmesan hails from the north, this is the cheese often used for grating in Southern Italy.

Cook the pasta according to the packet's instructions, then drain and toss in 3 tablespoons of olive oil.

Meanwhile, boil the asparagus until just tender; this should take 4–6 minutes depending on thickness. Drain and plunge into cold water, then pat dry.

Grate 100g (3½oz) of the Pecorino. Add the asparagus to the pasta with the pesto and grated Pecorino. Toss well and season to taste with salt and pepper.

Allow to cool, tossing occasionally. Once cool, it might need a little more oil. If so, toss in 1 tablespoon. Then 'shave' the remaining Pecorino and pile this on top. Serve at room temperature with a garnish of fresh basil.

PALM HEART SALAD WITH ORANGE JUICE & HONEY

Serves 3–4

400g (14oz) tin of palm hearts, drained

3 tablespoons freshly squeezed orange juice

1 teaspoon honey

Salt and freshly ground black pepper

1 tablespoon fresh coriander

Everywhere you travel in Latin American, you find palm heart salad – 'palmitos' are the one ubiquitous vegetable, if we can indeed label them thus. I have eaten them in Brazil, Venezuela and Chile in salads; and I believe that in the Dominican Republic they are stewed with tomatoes and peppers and served with grated cheese on top. Because of their distinctive texture and flavour, they are usually served very simply – with either tomatoes or avocados, and perhaps with a sprinkling of fresh coriander. In one street café on the Copacabana in Rio, I was served a huge plateful of palm hearts and nothing else. A large canister of olive oil was plonked down beside the plate and that was it. But, I have to say, they tasted pretty good – unless I was also affected by the vibrant atmosphere, with samba dancers limbering up nearby and sun-worshipping bodies gyrating to the frantic music on the beach. Oh, and did I mention one or two lethal 'caipirinhas' just to set the scene?

Lay the drained palm hearts out on a serving dish. Place the orange juice and honey in a small saucepan and slowly bring to the boil. Then remove, season well and pour over the palm hearts. Once cool, roughly tear the coriander leaves and scatter over the top. Serve at room temperature.

CLASSIC WALDORF SALAD

Serves 6

6 sticks of celery, chopped

75g (2¾oz) walnuts, shelled

2 large red or green-skinned crisp apples, unpeeled, chopped

The juice of 1 lemon

3 tablespoons mayonnaise (see page 154)

2 tablespoons Greek yoghurt

Salt and freshly ground black pepper

This classic dish is so good, with its contrasting flavours and textures and its unsurpassable crunch, that you might think you cannot better it. I have, however, developed the Waldorf idea a little, so try both this traditional recipe and my alternative version which follows.

Place the celery and nuts in a bowl. Toss the apple in the lemon juice and add with the mayonnaise and yoghurt. Season well, toss together and serve.

WALDORF SALAD WITH PEARS & BRAZIL NUTS

Serves 6

6 sticks of celery, chopped

75g (2¾oz) brazil nuts, shelled

2 large ripe yet firm pears, unskinned, chopped

The juice of 1 lemon

3 tablespoons mayonnaise (see page 154)

2 tablespoons Greek yoghurt

Salt and freshly ground black pepper

My contribution to the Waldorf salad is to use pears and brazil nuts instead of the usual walnuts and apples. You may indeed prefer it.

Place the celery and nuts in a bowl. Toss the pears in the lemon juice and add to the bowl with the mayonnaise and yoghurt. Season well, then toss together and serve.

SICILIAN AUBERGINE SALAD

Serves 4–6

2 large aubergines, wiped, cut into
2.5 cm (1 in) chunks

6 tablespoons olive oil

1 onion, peeled, chopped

2 garlic cloves, peeled, chopped

4 plum tomatoes, chopped

1 tablespoon granulated sugar

2 level tablespoons sun-dried
tomatoes, chopped

2 heaped tablespoons capers,
drained

4 tablespoons red wine vinegar

Salt and freshly ground
black pepper

2 heaped tablespoons freshly
chopped flat-leaf parsley

This is a cold aubergine dish very loosely based on the Sicilian 'Caponata', a dish of fried onions, celery and aubergines that are then simmered in a sweet and sour sauce. My recipe is similar, but features primarily aubergines, and only capers rather than the usual combination of olives and capers. I also like to incorporate some sun-dried tomatoes for their texture and added flavour. I then strew it abundantly with parsley just before serving, to balance the sweetness a little. If your sun-dried tomatoes are preserved in extra virgin olive oil, then use some of the oil to cook the onions and garlic.

Cook the aubergines in 4 tablespoons of oil in a wide saucepan for about 5 minutes until just turning brown. Tip them into a bowl and add the remaining oil to the pan. Fry the onion and garlic for about 5 minutes, then add the tomatoes, granulated sugar and sun-dried tomatoes. Stirring constantly until the sugar has completely dissolved, cook over a gentle heat for about 5 minutes.

Return the aubergines to the pan with the capers and vinegar and cook, covered, over a medium heat for about 15 minutes, or until tender. Season according to taste, then tip into a bowl and cool. (Leave overnight if you prefer.) Just before serving, scatter the chopped flat-leaf parsley over the top.

Quinoa with Roasted Onions

Serves 4

2 onions

3 tablespoons olive oil

175g (6oz) quinoa

2 fat garlic cloves, peeled, chopped

300ml (½ pint) hot chicken stock

2 heaped tablespoons freshly
chopped mint

½ tablespoon red wine vinegar

Salt and freshly ground
black pepper

Quinoa is a high-protein grain indigenous to the Andes. Because of its blobby, vaguely tapioca-like texture, some people might not like it at first. But, depending on what it is cooked with, it has enormous potential. Here it is served with roasted onions and plenty of fresh mint to make an unusual salad that is an ideal accompaniment to roast or barbecued meat.

Preheat the oven to 200°C/400°F/gas mark 6. Cut the top off the onions and carefully level off the base, without actually cutting it away – this is to keep the sections in place once you have quartered them. Then peel the onions and cut vertically into quarters. Place in a tight-fitting roasting tin with 1 tablespoon of oil. Roast for about 1 hour, or until tender and golden brown.

Rinse the quinoa, then heat the remaining oil in a saucepan. Gently fry the garlic for 2–3 minutes, then stir in the quinoa. After 1 minute, add the hot stock, stir well and bring to the boil. Season and cover. Reduce to a simmer and cook for about 20 minutes, until all the liquid has evaporated.

Then tip the quinoa into a bowl and stir in the mint, vinegar and salt and pepper to taste. Add the onion quarters and the oil from the roasting tin. Stir very gently to avoid breaking up the onion quarters and serve at room temperature with perhaps an extra shake of wine vinegar.

ELEPHANT FOOT BREAD WITH AVO SALAD

Serves 6

FOR THE BREAD

300g (10½oz) potatoes (unpeeled weight), peeled, halved

25g (1oz) unsalted butter

450g (1lb) strong white bread flour

6g (¼oz) sachet of easy-blend dried yeast

Approximately 350ml (12floz) hand-hot water (one-third boiling water mixed with two-thirds cold)

1 tablespoon salt

2 teaspoons caraway seeds

FOR THE AVO SALAD

2 avocados, peeled, sliced

2 plum tomatoes, sliced

The juice of 1 lime

2 tablespoons extra virgin olive oil

Salt and freshly ground black pepper

On a trip to South Africa I was fortunate enough to stay in a fabulous game reserve which had a terrific local chef. One of her specialities was Elephant Foot Bread, so-called because of its shape. When making this, just think Large. I have reduced the quantity of the dough for my recipe as my oven is not quite large enough for an elephant's foot, but my bread is still an impressive size. I like to serve it with the same chef's avocado salad recipe.

For the bread, boil the potatoes until tender, then mash with the butter until soft. This should be done only when you are ready to start the bread as it is important that the potatoes are still warm when you mix them.

While they are boiling, mix about 100g (3½oz) of the flour with the yeast in a bowl, then stir in 100ml (3½floz) hand-hot water. Once combined, leave for 20 minutes.

Then mix the remaining flour into this 'starter' with the salt, caraway and remaining water (you might not need it all). You are aiming for a soft but not sticky consistency. With floured hands, transfer to a floured board and knead for about 10 minutes until the dough is supple and smooth. Then shape into a ball and place in an oiled bowl. Cover and leave somewhere warm (such as an airing cupboard) for 1–2 hours until well risen.

Preheat the oven to 220°C/425°F/gas mark 7. Knock back the dough (which means literally punch it to deflate it slightly), then drop it – in a vaguely elephant foot-like shape – onto an oiled baking tray. Bake in the oven for 20 minutes, reduce the temperature to 190°C/375°F/gas mark 5 and bake for a further 15–20 minutes until done. Test by tapping the underside – it should sound hollow. Allow to cool before serving with the salad.

Arrange the avocados and tomatoes on a plate. Drizzle over the lime juice and oil with plenty of salt and pepper.

WATERCRESS & RED PEPPER SALAD

Serves 4

1 large bunch of watercress, washed

2 red peppers, grilled, skinned, slivered (see page 97)

2 tablespoons pumpkin seed oil

1 tablespoon sunflower oil

1 tablespoon red wine vinegar

Salt and freshly ground black pepper

Toasted pumpkin seeds, optional (see page 92)

Pumpkin seed oil is used in the dressing in this bright and cheerful salad. Its distinctive nutty taste is good in many salads, but I always like to 'thin' it down with a neutral oil such as sunflower oil, otherwise it can be overwhelming.

Place the watercress in a bowl, then top with the red pepper slivers. Mix together the oils and vinegar and season well. Pour over the salad, toss then serve at once, topped with pumpkin seeds, if desired.

MOROCCAN ORANGE SALAD

Serves 4–6

3 large oranges

½ red onion, peeled, finely sliced

2 heaped tablespoons freshly chopped flat-leaf parsley

1 heaped tablespoon freshly chopped coriander

Salt and freshly ground black pepper

1 tablespoon orange juice

Few drops of orange blossom water (optional)

This salad looks spectacular. And it tastes rather good, too. It is refreshing, aromatic and fun. Serve it at barbecues or with any grilled or roast meats or fish. If you can get hold of it, do sprinkle over some orange blossom water, to enhance the entire orange flavour (see right).

Peel and slice the oranges and remove all the white pith. If there are any pips, remove these too. Lay the oranges in a shallow dish.

Mix together the onion, parsley and coriander and season with salt and pepper. Sprinkle over the oranges, then pour over the orange juice (and orange water if using). Leave to stand for at least 1 hour before serving at room temperature.

BLACK-EYED BEAN SALAD

Serves 6

250g (9oz) black-eyed beans

3 tablespoons olive oil

1 tablespoon red wine vinegar

1 orange or red pepper

2–3 plum tomatoes, diced

3–4 tablespoons freshly chopped
flat-leafed parsley

2 garlic cloves, peeled, crushed

2–3 spring onions, sliced diagonally

Salt and freshly ground
black pepper

Black-eyed beans, although native to China, are now used throughout the world, and are particularly popular in the southern States of America, where they are mixed with rice and used in dishes of salt pork and beans. They are also found in West African and Caribbean kitchens. You can substitute coriander for the parsley and add a chopped red chilli and a shake of soy sauce for a more eastern flavour, if you wish. Allow time for soaking the beans overnight (see left).

Soak the beans overnight, then rinse well and cook them in plenty of boiling water according to the packet's instructions. Drain well.

While they are still warm, mix them with the oil and vinegar, then, once cool, stir through the remaining ingredients. Season to taste and serve at room temperature.

SOUTH AMERICAN SALAD

Serves 4

4 large tomatoes, chopped

1 small red onion, peeled, finely
chopped

3 tablespoons olive oil

15g (½oz) freshly chopped
coriander

Salt and freshly ground
black pepper

This is a common salad in Chile, where it is served with the copious amounts of grilled meat that are served in that beautiful mountainous country, and indeed everywhere else on the continent. Vegetarians would, I fear, have a difficult time in South America.

Combine everything together in a bowl and stir in plenty of salt and pepper to taste. Serve at room temperature.

Turkish Aubergine with Mint Yoghurt

Serves 6

2 large aubergines, sliced thickly

Salt and freshly ground
black pepper

4–6 tablespoons olive oil

400ml (14fl oz) Greek yoghurt

The juice of 1 lemon

2 tablespoons fresh mint, plus extra
to garnish

2 garlic cloves, peeled, finely
chopped

This is based on a Turkish dish I used to eat nearly every night as part of a huge 'mezze' table during a holiday in western Turkey. Thick Greek yoghurt is ideal for this dish, which should be served chilled with warm flat bread.

Salt the aubergines and leave for about 30 minutes to extract the bitter juices, then rinse off the salt and pat dry.

Heat the olive oil in a frying pan and fry the aubergines in two batches until golden brown and tender. Drain them on kitchen paper.

In a bowl, beat together the yoghurt, lemon juice, mint, garlic and plenty of salt and pepper. Once the aubergines are cool, place on a shallow serving plate and spoon over the yoghurt mixture. Chill until served.

Gherkin, Ham, Dill & Feta Salad

Serves 4

4 large gherkins, chopped

75g (2¾oz) quality roast ham or
gammon, diced

3 heaped tablespoons freshly
chopped dill

150g (5½oz) Feta cheese, chopped

1 red pepper, grilled, chopped
(see page 97)

2 tablespoons olive oil

Freshly ground black pepper

This is another Turkish-inspired salad and has some gloriously strident flavours with salty tangy feta, sour gherkins and fresh aniseed-like dill. Mix everything together gently so the cheese does not break up too much.

Mix the first five ingredients gently together in a bowl and drizzle over the olive oil. Add plenty of ground pepper – no salt, as the cheese is already salty. Serve at room temperature.

WILTED CABBAGE WITH OLIVE OIL & PANCETTA

Serves 4–6

4 tablespoons extra virgin olive oil

75g (2¾oz) pancetta, cubed

3 garlic cloves, peeled, chopped

450g (1lb) cabbage, sliced

Worcestershire sauce

1 tablespoon sherry vinegar

Salt and freshly ground
black pepper

It is important to use a good, preferably fruity olive oil for this dish. As the dish is served at room temperature – neither hot nor cold – the flavour really does come through. Use either white cabbage or one of the dark green varieties. Serve with roast meats or as a vegetarian main course, perhaps with a little crumbled feta or blue cheese sprinkled over the top.

Heat the oil in a saucepan for about 1 minute, then add the pancetta and garlic. Fry over a medium heat for about 10 minutes until the pancetta is just turning crispy. Add the cabbage and a good dash of Worcestershire sauce. Stirring well to coat in the oil, let the cabbage cook over a medium-high heat for 3–5 minutes, or until it has wilted and is just beginning to soften. Remove from the heat and add the vinegar. Season to taste with salt and pepper and allow to cool to room temperature before serving.

CORIANDER & MINT CHUTNEY

Serves 4–6

50g (1¾oz) desiccated coconut

5 tablespoons coconut milk
(from a tin)

15g (½oz) fresh coriander

15g (½oz) fresh mint

½ red chilli, chopped

200ml (7fl oz) Greek yoghurt

The juice of ½ lemon

Salt and freshly ground
black pepper

This chutney recipe is based on one I learned to make in the Delhi kitchen of chef Gev Desai. His 'hara' (green chutney) is simply a mixture of coriander, green chillies, mint and a little cumin. He sometimes adds optional extras such as coconut or yoghurt. I think that they lessen the fiery bite of the chilli somewhat. Do, by all means, increase the amount of chilli in this recipe – Gev uses a great deal more, to suit local tastes. Serve this chutney as a dip for pakoras or smeared over oven-baked fish. It is also good served with fish cakes or good old fish and chips.

Soak the coconut in the coconut milk for 20–30 minutes. Place the remaining ingredients in a food processor and add the soaked coconut. Whizz until blended, then taste and add salt and pepper accordingly.

TABBOULEH WITH FRIED PARMA HAM

Serves 6

200g (7oz) bulgar wheat, rinsed

20g (¾oz) freshly chopped
flat-leaf parsley

20g (¾oz) freshly chopped mint

4–5 spring onions, finely chopped

3 plum tomatoes, finely chopped

½ cucumber, finely chopped

4 tablespoons olive oil

The juice of 1 large lemon

2 teaspoons salt

Freshly ground black pepper

Chicory leaves, to serve

100g (3½oz) Parma ham

When served tabbouleh in this county, you are often given an enormous pile of bulgar wheat dotted with a minuscule amount of tomatoes and herbs. You might be surprised at the ratio of wheat to 'other bits' in my recipe, but you should bear in mind that the stars of the show are traditionally the parsley, tomatoes and mint, not the bulgar (often written 'burghul'). And believe me, it is not only more authentic this way, it tastes divine. The authenticity grinds to a halt when we come to the garnish. You are unlikely to find fried Parma ham in the tabboulehs of Cairo or Beirut, but it does make a good garnish, the salty flavour and crispy texture complementing the salad perfectly. Eat this as they do in the Middle East, with salad leaves to scoop up the tabbouleh. You can use cos or little gems, but I prefer chicory.

Place the wheat in a wide, shallow bowl and cover with about 500ml (18floz) boiling water. Cover and leave to stand for at least 20 minutes.

Then drain off any excess water, making sure there is no liquid left. Tip in the parsley, mint, onions, tomatoes and cucumber and stir well. Pour over the oil and lemon juice and stir in the salt. Season well with pepper and, once well combined, taste and check seasoning.

Line a shallow salad bowl with the chicory leaves and tip the tabbouleh in.

Just before serving, heat a non-stick pan to hot and add the Parma ham (without added fat). Fry for 3–4 minutes, turning once, until crispy. Tip the ham while still warm over the salad and serve at once.

CHILLI BEEF & CORNBREAD

Serves 6

FOR THE CORNBREAD

300g (10½oz) plain flour

1 level tablespoon baking powder

150g (5½oz) fine polenta
(I use 'quick-cook' polenta, ready
in 5 minutes)

1 teaspoon salt

225ml (8floz) milk

75g (3oz) unsalted butter, melted

2 free-range eggs, beaten

40g (1½oz) caster sugar

3 tablespoons corn kernels
(from a can)

½–1 green chilli, deseeded, finely
chopped (add more to taste)

1 green chilli, deseeded, chopped

1 teaspoon ground cumin

1 teaspoon freeze-dried oregano

4–5 spring onions, chopped

The juice of 1 large lime

2 garlic cloves, peeled, chopped

½ teaspoon salt

1 tablespoon sunflower oil

500g (1lb 2oz) rump beef, cut into
strips

Salt and freshly ground
black pepper

2 avocados, sliced

Wedges of lime, to serve

150ml (5floz) sour cream

This is a dish inspired by south-western cooking in the United States. There you find many Mexican flavours marry with local ingredients such as beef, pine nuts or cactus paddles – the edible, fleshy green leaves of the nopal cactus. My cornbread recipe here, studded with corn kernels and green chilli, is a variation of those I ate on a visit to Phoenix, Arizona. The beef is stir-fried with Mexican flavourings and served warm with a hunk of the cornbread, some avocado slices, wedges of lime and a dish of sour cream to dollop on top of the beef.

Preheat the oven to 220°C/425°F/gas mark 7. For the cornbread, sift together the flour and baking powder and stir in the polenta and salt. Beat the milk and butter together.

Whisk together the eggs and sugar and add, with the milk mixture, to the bowl containing the polenta. Stir in the corn and chilli, then tip into a greased 23cm (9in) square tin. Bake for 25–30 minutes until risen and golden. Cool in the tin for at least 30 minutes, then turn out and serve warm, cut into hunks. (It can be reheated in a low oven loosely covered with foil or very briefly in a microwave.)

Meanwhile, place the chilli, cumin, oregano, onions, lime juice, garlic and salt in a grinder or small blender. Whizz until thoroughly combined.

Heat up a frying pan, then add the oil. Once it is hot, add the chilli paste and fry for 1 minute, stirring continually, then add the beef and fry for about 3 minutes, stirring well, over a high heat. Check seasoning once ready.

To serve, place the avocado slices around a shallow serving plate and sprinkle lightly with lemon juice. Tip the beef with its juices into the middle of the plate. Arrange some lime wedges around the side of the plate. Just before serving, spoon some sour cream on top and serve with hunks of warm cornbread.

COURGETTE ROLLS WITH MINT

Serves 6

4 courgettes, trimmed, wiped

5–6 tablespoons olive oil

5 heaped tablespoons fresh mint

25g (1oz) pine nuts

25g (1oz) freshly grated
Parmesan cheese

1 garlic clove, peeled, chopped

Salt and freshly ground
black pepper

Sprigs of mint, to decorate
(optional)

These little courgette rolls stuffed with a tangy mint pesto make an ideal dish for a buffet table. Drizzled with a little extra olive oil and served with perhaps a little rocket salad, they make an interesting starter, too. They can also – provided they are smallish – be served as canapés. But do supply napkins. Aubergines also work well in this recipe, but grill them for a shorter time.

Preheat the grill. Cut the courgettes lengthwise into about four slices each and place on a grill tray. Brush with 1–2 tablespoons of oil and grill for 8–10 minutes on each side or until tender and golden brown. Then remove and place on kitchen paper to drain.

Meanwhile, place the mint, pine nuts, Parmesan and garlic in a food processor and process briefly, then add 4 tablespoons of oil and process again. Season to taste, then tip into a bowl.

To assemble, spread one heaped teaspoon of the mixture over each courgette slice and roll up, starting at the narrow end. Place these on a serving dish and decorate with sprigs of mint, if you wish.

SWEDISH HERRING & BEETROOT SALAD

Serves 4

250 g (9 oz) jar of Swedish marinated herring, diced

6 slices of pickled beetroot, patted dry, diced

1 crisp red apple, unpeeled, diced

2 teaspoons horseradish sauce

1 tablespoon mayonnaise (see page 154)

2 tablespoons natural yoghurt

Salt and freshly ground black pepper

3–4 handfuls red chard leaves (or young spinach)

This is a lovely colourful salad that makes a welcome addition to any cold buffet. If you can find it, do try to use red chard for the salad leaves, as its colour and flavour blends in beautifully. Alternatively, use young spinach. The herring can be found already marinated in jars, and sometimes with dill or white wine marinades. These are fine, but avoid any that have a sour cream or thick mustard dressing. Rollmops will also work very well here. Try to cut the herring, beetroot and apple into the same size of dice.

Place the herring, beetroot and apple in a bowl and gently mix with the horseradish, mayonnaise and yoghurt. Season with salt and pepper to taste. Place the red chard leaves in a salad bowl and pile the mixture on top. Gently toss everything together and serve at room temperature, with Swedish-style rye bread and butter.

THE SWEET HEREAFTER

*I have always loved fresh fruit salads – probably because
I absolutely adore fresh fruit. But I must confess, when they are
served as puddings, I do insist on a liberal sloshing of cream,
thick yoghurt or – my all-time favourite – home-made vanilla
ice-cream, made with dark, sticky vanilla pods. But that's just
me and my inherent sweet tooth; to me, a pudding is not a
pudding unless I end up feeling vaguely guilty and self-
indulgent afterwards.*

*Here are several recipes for sweet salads, hot and cold, which
can be served as they are, healthy and sensible. They mainly
consist of fruit but also use nuts, dried fruit and sweetmeats
such as marshmallows and Turkish delight – not forgetting
chocolate of course. They are even more satisfying served with
a dollop of your favourite accompaniment, whether it is cream,
yoghurt or ice-cream. I have been known to have all three.*

STRAWBERRY, MANGO & CHAMPAGNE SALAD

Serves 4

400g (14oz) strawberries, halved
or quartered

2 large ripe mangoes, cubed

The seeds and juice of
½ pomegranate

1 large glass champagne or
sparkling wine

This is one for special occasions! And although you might normally buy only dry champagne, this recipe tastes even better with a medium or slightly sweet champagne or sparkling wine. It should be served immediately the fizz is poured over and without any adornments such as cream.

Place the strawberries, mangoes and pomegranate in a pretty glass bowl.

Just before serving, pour over the wine and serve at once, while you can still hear the bubbles hissing.

PAPAYA, MANGO & PASSIONFRUIT SALAD

Serves 6

2 large papayas, cubed

2 large mangoes, cubed

6 passionfruit, halved

1 heaped tablespoon golden
caster sugar

This salad is also good tipped out into a flattish serving dish and topped with a layer of thick yoghurt. Sprinkle over a layer of dark muscovado sugar, chill for a couple of hours then serve (see left).

Combine the papaya and mango in a glass bowl. Scoop the pulp of each passionfruit into a small saucepan and add the sugar. Heat gently until warm, then press the mixture through a sieve over the bowl of fruit. Stir everything together, then scatter the passionfruit seeds over the top. Serve chilled.

STRAWBERRY & MARSHMALLOW SALAD

Serves 4–6

300 g (10½ oz) strawberries, halved
or quartered

300 g (10½ oz) seedless grapes

50 g (1¾ oz) mini marshmallows

3 tablespoons freshly squeezed
orange juice

I know what you're thinking: marshmallows in a fruit salad? She can't be serious. But this is in fact a fun dessert that has its origins in – guess where – The States. Be sure to chill well before serving (see right).

Place all the ingredients in a glass bowl and toss gently. Leave covered in the refrigerator for at least 3 hours before serving.

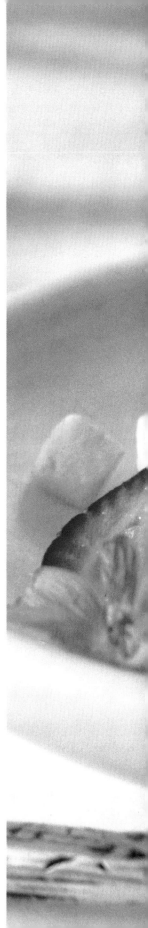

MANGO & PAPAYA STIR-FRY

Serves 4

1 tablespoon sunflower oil

2 teaspoons light muscovado sugar

2 teaspoons freshly grated ginger

1 large mango, peeled, cubed

1 large papaya, halved,
deseeded, cubed

A sweet stir-fry might sound a little unconventional, but this is actually delicious. It is best served warm but also tastes good cold. Serve with thick yoghurt.

Heat the oil in large frying pan or wok. Add the sugar and ginger and heat over a medium heat until the sugar has dissolved. Then increase the heat and add the mango and papaya. Stirring gently, cook over a high heat for 2–3 minutes until piping hot. Tip into a serving bowl.

RASPBERRIES WITH WHITE CHOCOLATE & PINE NUTS

Serves 3

25g (1oz) pine nuts

250g (9oz) raspberries

25g (1oz) quality white chocolate

The combination of raspberries and white chocolate is a match made in heaven. The combination of raspberries and pine nuts is also very good. And all three together? Unforgettable! (See right.)

Heat the nuts in a non-stick frying pan for 2–3 minutes until light golden brown. Shake the pan around so they do not burn. Tip onto kitchen paper to cool.

Place the raspberries in a glass bowl and top with the cooled nuts. Either coarsely grate or shave the chocolate, then scatter over the top. Serve chilled.

TROPICAL FRUIT SALAD

Serves 4–6

1 large mango, peeled, chopped

1 large papaya, peeled, chopped

3 kiwi fruit, peeled, sliced

½ large (or 1 medium) pineapple, peeled, chopped

1 star fruit, sliced

4 passionfruit

The juice of 1 lemon

This is an extremely versatile recipe. Add whichever tropical fruit you can get your hands on. Do try to find passion fruit to use as the dressing, however, as the tiny seeds look stunning throughout the salad. Serve with pouring cream.

Gently mix the first five ingredients together in a bowl. Cut each passionfruit in half and scoop out the juice and pulp into a food processor. Add the lemon juice and whizz until combined. Pour this over the salad and toss gently to combine. Serve chilled.

PLUM & ORANGE COMPOTE WITH CINNAMON SHORTBREAD

Serves 4–6

500g (1 lb 2oz) plums, stoned, quartered

40g (1½oz) light brown sugar

The grated zest and juice of 1 large orange

FOR THE SHORTBREAD

200g (7oz) slightly salted butter, slightly softened

100g (3½oz) golden caster sugar

175g (6oz) plain flour, sifted

28g (1oz) semolina

1 heaped teaspoon ground cinnamon

2–3 teaspoons demerara sugar

A warm plum compote is served with crisp, buttery shortbread in this lovely autumnal dessert. If you have never made shortbread before, just remember that overhandling the dough will result in tough biscuits. Ignore any shortbread recipes that ask you to knead the dough for 5 minutes – these were obviously not written by a Scot. Serve accompanied with thick cream.

For the compote, place everything in a saucepan and bring slowly to the boil. Cover, reduce to a simmer and cook for about 10–15 minutes, or until the plums are soft but not mushy. The length of time will depend on the ripeness of the plums.

Preheat the oven to 160°C/325°F/gas mark 3. For the shortbread, cream together the butter and caster sugar, using a wooden spoon. Stir in the flour, semolina and cinnamon. Using floured hands, combine into a ball and gently pat out onto a lightly floured board, until you have a thinnish rectangle. Using a pastry cutter, cut out about 20 little biscuits and place on two lightly buttered baking trays, spacing the biscuits apart, as they tend to spread. Sprinkle over the demerara sugar.

Bake in the oven for about 25 minutes, or until firm but not colouring too much. Remove and leave for a couple of minutes, then transfer to a wire tray to cool completely.

Serve with the warm compote.

Rhubarb & Vanilla Compote with Fried Semolina

Serves 4

FOR THE SEMOLINA

500 ml (18 fl oz) creamy milk

50 g (1¾ oz) semolina

75 g (2¾ oz) golden caster sugar

25 g (1 oz) unsalted butter, plus extra for greasing

FOR THE COMPOTE

600 g (1 lb 5 oz) young rhubarb, washed, chopped

50 g (1¾ oz) golden caster sugar

1 vanilla pod, split

Remember school semolina with a splodge of bright red jam? Remember swirling it round and round until the entire dish was lurid pink? Yum, I loved it. But did you also have stewed rhubarb with your school semolina? What a waste of good semolina; what a waste of good rhubarb, the way they cooked it. But if you think about it, the combination is perfect: the tartness of the rhubarb balancing the thick creamy semolina. When the first of the young rhubarb appears in the shops at the end of winter, I long to rustle up semolina and rhubarb. And sometimes, I serve the semolina cooked, chilled until set, then fried in butter and sugar. The result is a slightly caramelised semolina served with a lovely vanilla-flavoured compote. It is the stuff of dreams ... which certainly cannot be said of school dinner rhubarb.

First, make the semolina. Bring the milk to the boil, then add the semolina and 50 g (1¾ oz) sugar. Stirring constantly, cook over a medium heat for about 15 minutes until thick. Pour into a buttered 18–20 cm (7–8 in) square baking tray and leave to cool, then refrigerate overnight.

Next day, cut into four (squares, rectangles or diamonds). Slowly heat the butter and remaining sugar in a frying pan. Once the sugar has melted, increase the heat to medium and fry the semolina pieces (you may need to do this in two batches) for about 3 minutes on each side, or until golden brown and caramelised. Turn them carefully so they do not break.

For the compote, place everything in a saucepan and bring slowly to the boil. Boil, uncovered, for about 5 minutes, or until the rhubarb is tender. Cover and leave to stand for at least 30 minutes.

To serve, place one piece of warm semolina on a plate and spoon some warm compote on the side.

Scandinavian Fruit Soup

Serves 4

500 g (1 lb 2 oz) berries
(strawberries and raspberries
are best, but use
a mixture and add some
blueberries, stoned cherries or
even chopped rhubarb)

250 ml (9 fl oz) fruit juice
(orange, apple or cranberry)

15 g (½ oz) potato flour (available
in health-food shops; or
use arrowroot)

25 g (1 oz) golden caster sugar

There are many forms of fruit soups served throughout Scandinavia. In Sweden, there is 'Blandad fruktsoppa', a dried fruit soup thickened with potato flour or tapioca. In Denmark, 'Frugtsuppe' is made with apples, pears, elderberries, strawberries or any other fruits country folk would gather from hedgerows or gardens. Again, it is usually thickened with potato flour or sometimes with rice, sago or semolina. But it is the Finnish fruit soup 'Vatkattu marjapuuro', thickened with semolina, which I am most familiar with. The direct translation from Finnish is Whipped Berry Porridge, for porridge is to the Finns what steamed pudding and custard are to the British. It is summed up in two words: comfort food. The soft, light yet full-bodied flavour of the porridge arouses the usually taciturn Finn to odes of joy. Usually made from their most commonly used berry, the lingonberry, it can also be made from the other typical berries, such as blueberries, brambles, cranberries or rosehips. Some Finns say that if you have any sort of stomach complaint, a quick dose of blueberry soup will set everything right. It certainly beats the annoying hiss and froth of Alkaseltzers in my book. Serve with a splash of creamy milk or single cream, Finnish-style.

Place all but 100 g (3½ oz) fruit in a liquidiser with the fruit juice and process well, then push through a sieve over a saucepan.

Bring the mixture slowly to the boil. In a bowl, mix together the potato flour and 4 teaspoons of cold water to make a smooth paste. Gradually add this to the pan, stirring all the time, and cook over a gentle heat (do not boil) for about 5 minutes or until thick. Add the sugar (you may need more depending on the type of fruit used) and the remaining berries (whole or halved if large). Stir, then tip into a glass bowl. Allow to cool, stirring occasionally to prevent a skin forming. Serve cold.

WARM FUDGEY CHOCOLATE CAKE WITH FRUIT SALSA

Serves 8

FOR THE CAKE

300g (10½oz) dark chocolate (55%–70% cocoa solids)

150g (5½oz) unsalted butter

150g (5½oz) caster sugar

4 medium free-range eggs, separated

40g (1½oz) plain flour, sifted

Pinch of salt

FOR THE SALSA

400g (14oz) strawberries, diced

3 peaches, peeled, stoned, diced

1 tablespoon orange juice

This cake can be made in advance and reheated in a low oven, loosely covered in foil. It rises as it cooks then deflates slightly as it cools, forming a lovely soft fudgey centre. Serve wedges of the cake warm, with the chilled salsa and a dollop of clotted cream.

Preheat the oven to 180°C/350°F/gas mark 4. Butter and base-line a 24cm (9½in) springform cake tin.

For the cake, melt the chocolate, butter and sugar slowly together in a bowl set over a pan of simmering water, or in a microwave on medium. Remove from the heat and stir well. Leave for at least 5 minutes, then stir in the eggs yolks, one at a time.

Whisk the egg whites until they form soft peaks. Fold the flour, a pinch of salt and a little of the egg white into the chocolate mixture, then gradually fold in the remaining egg whites.

Pour the mixture into the prepared tin. Tap gently to level out, then bake in the oven for 35 minutes. Remove and allow to cool in the tin for at least 20 minutes before decanting and serving warm. (Alternatively, cool completely in the tin then reheat in a low oven, loosely wrapped in foil, prior to serving.)

For the salsa, mix the strawberries, peaches and juice very gently together. Refrigerate until serving with the cake.

FRUIT SALAD CRUNCHY CRUMBLE

Serves 4–6

250g (9oz) dried fruit salad

3 tablespoons orange juice

2 tablespoons dark muscovado sugar

4 bananas, thickly sliced

FOR THE TOPPING

100g (3½oz) plain flour, sifted

50g (1¾oz) unsalted butter, diced

50g (1¾oz) dark muscovado sugar

50g (1¾oz) porridge oats

50g (1¾oz) pecans or walnuts, roughly chopped

3 tablespoons sunflower oil

This is a mixture of dried fruit and bananas topped with an oaty, nutty crumble. If you cannot find a packet of ready-mixed dried fruit salad, then use a mixture of dried apricots, pears, apples and any tropical dried fruit such as mango or papaya. Serve with some Greek yoghurt or thick cream.

Cut up any large dried fruit (such as the pears) and soak them all in the orange juice for at least 1 hour.

Tip the fruit and juice into an ovenproof dish and sprinkle over 2 tablespoons of sugar. Top with the bananas.

Preheat the oven to 200°C/ 400°F/gas mark 6. For the topping, place the flour in a bowl and rub in the butter. Then stir in the remaining sugar, the oats, nuts and oil. Stir, then tip over the fruit and press gently down. Bake for 40–45 minutes until golden brown. Serve warm.

DRIED APRICOT & PEAR COMPOTE WITH GINGER

Serves 6

250g (9oz) dried apricots

250g (9oz) dried pears

300ml (10floz) orange juice

2 Earl Grey tea-bags

2 teaspoons honey

2 balls of stem ginger (from a jar
of ginger in syrup), chopped

This dish can be served warm as pudding, with a scoop of home-made vanilla or cinnamon ice-cream; or cold for breakfast, perhaps with some thick yoghurt over muesli or porridge.

Place the fruits in a saucepan with the juice and tea-bags. Bring to the boil, then when bubbles appear, remove from the heat and cover. Leave to stand for about 1 hour, then remove the tea-bags, add the honey and ginger and bring back to the boil. Simmer for about 10 minutes, then tip into a dish and serve either warm or cold.

FIG, ROSEMARY & PISTACHIO COMPOTE

Serves 4

250g (9oz) dried figs

2 sprigs of freshly chopped
rosemary

2 teaspoons rosewater

2 teaspoons caster sugar

50g (1¾oz) natural (unsalted)
pistachios, shelled, roughly chopped

Dried figs are not everybody's cup of tea. But enhanced with exotic flavourings such as rosewater, rosemary and pistachios, they come into their own in this delightful compote which is good either for breakfast or as an unusual pudding, accompanied by a good dollop of Greek yoghurt.

Snip the tough stalks from the figs and place the figs in a saucepan with the rosemary, 100ml (3½floz) water, rosewater and sugar. Heat gently until the sugar dissolves, then increase to high and bubble for about 4–5 minutes until slightly syrupy. Remove and cool, then stir in the pistachios. Serve cold and add an extra drop or 2 of rosewater, if you like.

CLASSIC FRUIT SALAD

Serves 4–6

3 nectarines or peaches, sliced with the peel left on

½ honeydew melon, cut into chunks

1 crisp apple, unpeeled and cut into chunks

3 tablespoons freshly squeezed orange juice

200g (7oz) raspberries

Some people do not believe a fruit salad is complete without banana. If you are of this opinion, then add just one small slice of banana just before serving to avoid it turning brown. When you are cutting the juicy fruit – the melon and the mango – save the juices and pour into the salad bowl. Serve with pouring cream or thick yoghurt.

Mix together the nectarine, melon and apple with the orange juice in a pretty glass bowl. Add the raspberries and very gently toss through, taking care not to bruise the delicate raspberries.

Chill for about an hour, then serve.

TURKISH DELIGHT WITH PISTACHIOS

Serves 4–6

200g (7oz) Turkish Delight

100g (3½oz) unsalted pistachios

1 tablespoon rosewater

Unsprayed rose petals (optional)

This dessert is for the extremely sweet-toothed: those who swoon with delight at the sight of all those Middle Eastern or North African sweetmeats that glisten with honey or sticky sugar syrup and bulge with nuts and fruits. Be sure to buy good Turkish Delight, preferably different colours and with nuts if you like. Decorate with a few garden rose petals (thoroughly inspected for insects!) to make it even more exotic.

Slice the chunks of Turkish Delight into 2 or 3 slices. It is easiest to do this by dipping a sharp knife into a packet of icing sugar before slicing. Lay the slices on a shallow dish.

Roughly chop the nuts and scatter over the top, then drizzle over about 1 tablespoon rosewater or to taste. Finally, strew with rose petals. Serve chilled.

LETTUCES AND LEAVES

Today we have no excuse for serving up limp, uninteresting lettuce leaves. The salad sections of our supermarkets and greengrocers seem to grow larger by the day, offering an ever-increasing range of lettuces and salad leaves all year round. There is always something new to try, from the imported oriental leaves to the wide variety of fresh herbs and the rich, refreshing flavours of the lettuces from the Mediterranean. Colour, too, plays an important part, with leaves ranging from the palest of greens to deep, rich reds. It's always worth experimenting, so next time you are in the shops, try something different, something you have not eaten before.

LETTUCES

Cos or Romaine
These tall, crisp lettuces with firm green leaves and pale hearts are ideal for classic Caesar salads and for salads with thickish dressings. Used individually, the leaves are ideal for dipping.

Iceberg
To be frank, although this is one of the most common lettuces, to be found in every supermarket, this large, compact lettuce is a waste of time if you are looking for any sort of flavour – although it is terrific on crunch.

Little Gem
Perfect miniature lettuces with sweet, crisp leaves which keep extremely well. They are ideal for children.

Oak Leaf
Also known as 'Feuille de Chêne', this well-flavoured, deep bronze lettuce with a serrated leaf adds excellent taste and texture to a salad.

Frisée
This is the type of lettuce I remember most from my time in the south of France. Its jagged leaves annoy me slightly now, as they tend to get stuck in my throat, but the slightly bitter flavour and its fresh crispness still make it a great favourite. Dress with a fruity Provençal olive oil, red wine vinegar and Dijon mustard for a classic southern French salad.

Lollo Rosso
This is another salad leaf which has become a household name over the years. This Italian red lettuce has frilly, decorative leaves. Its green version (Lollo Biondo) also makes a good, if slightly undynamic-tasting, salad leaf.

Spinach
Although not usually classified as a lettuce or salad leaf, young or baby spinach is so much in vogue it has to have a mention. Healthy, versatile and gloriously green, it can be dressed with any number of oils and vinegars. The only drawback about spinach is the fact that it invariably sticks between the teeth. So say absolutely nothing after a spinach salad with your loved one until you have nipped off for a quick check for green teeth in the mirror.

SALAD LEAVES

Watercress

Watercress is one of our quintessentially British ingredients. And although it is now available all year round, it used to be one of the few leaves to cheer our salad bowls throughout the winter months. There are references to its being used for many centuries both in salads and also in invigorating soups and tonics. Since it does not keep (have you, too, thrown out many slimy past-their-sell-by-date packets of watercress?), it is best eaten within 24 hours of purchase. Bunched watercress should be thoroughly washed and dried before using. Its peppery flavour enhances all sorts of salads and is also good when very lightly cooked or wilted into scrambled eggs or omelettes. Wild watercress should only ever be picked from free-flowing, unpolluted streams; if in any doubt, buy from a greengrocer.

Lamb's Lettuce

Despite its name, this is a salad leaf rather than a proper lettuce. Also known as corn salad and in France as 'mâche', this has been cultivated for some time in France and Italy, particularly as a winter salad leaf, but now – like so many other leaves – is available all year. It has a delicate, fairly mild flavour and very pleasing soft texture. It is important to wash it very thoroughly – or ideally stand it in cold water for an hour or so – to draw out any of the sandy soil lurking in the roots.

Rocket

One of the earliest salad leaves of spring, rocket (also known as roquette, rucola or arugula, and in Greece and Cyprus as 'rokka') is one of the new designer leaves we simply cannot get enough of. With its piquant, peppery and rather nutty flavour and pretty frilly leaf, it adds a sense of freshness and, let's face it, trendiness, to any salad. Apart from good olive oil and sherry vinegar, it is also divine dressed with walnut oil and balsamic vinegar. It can be processed into pesto which can be thinned down with olive oil and drizzled over roasted vegetables or tomato salad. Rocket flowers are also a welcome addition to any salad, or toss them over a dish of pasta just before serving.

Sorrel

A form of sour dock, this soft, leafy green salad herb has a sharp, acidic yet wonderfully refreshing taste. Older, tougher leaves should not be used in salads, but should be reserved for sorrel soup. I recommend making this by cooking up half the sorrel then, when blending, adding the remaining sorrel so it purées to a vivid green colour. Otherwise, cooked sorrel tends to become sludgy brown all too quickly. Buckler leaf or French sorrel, whose leaves are rounder and more reminiscent of tiny arrow heads than the longer, spear-shaped leaves of common sorrel, is slightly less acidic and therefore good to use in all sorts of salads.

Purslane

I first came across purslane in Turkey, where it is used – as it is in many Mediterranean countries – in salads. It has fleshy, rounded green leaves which are fairly mild in flavour yet nicely succulent and crisp in texture. Like sorrel, purslane is high in oxalic acid and so should not be eaten regularly in large quantities. It is good dressed with thick Greek yoghurt thinned down with a little lemon juice and a splash of olive oil.

Chicory

Mostly imported from Belgium, where it is called Witloof and is almost the national vegetable, chicory has a welcome bitterness and crisp clean bite, which makes it good in many salads. Because of its shape, the leaves also make ideal dunkers for dips such as guacamole, hummus or taramasalata. Avoid chicory tinged with too much brown.

Radicchio

A member of the chicory family, this is an Italian favourite and is thankfully now widely available. It also has a fairly bitter flavour but there is a slight nutty edge to it, which, in my opinion, makes it the ideal vehicle for walnut or hazelnut oil-based salad dressings.

Fennel

Fennel bulb, with its unique aniseed flavour and marvellously crunchy texture, makes an ideal addition to any salad, particularly those accompanying fish dishes. Often called Florence fennel, the bulb arrived in Britain from Italy some three centuries ago. The fronds of the bulb can be used instead of the herb fennel. Fennel flowers are also good scattered over salads.

Nasturtium Leaves

Don't just walk past those nasturtiums in your garden. Use both the flowers (well shaken or lightly washed to remove any wildlife) and the leaves. The leaves have a lovely peppery flavour and good fleshy texture. Use them in salads or make sandwiches by spreading good bread thickly with cream cheese and topping with the leaves. For salads, you can either shred the leaves roughly or add small ones whole. If using the flowers, divide them into individual petals and dress with vinaigrette only at the very last minute to prevent the leaves wilting.

Red Chard

The tender young leaves of this member of the beet family have a mild flavour but an interesting texture. The red-stalked variety, known as rhubarb chard, adds a good flash of colour to any plain green salad.

Red Mustard

Red mustard leaves, with their mottled green and maroon leaves, have a hot, peppery and decidedly mustardy flavour. The baby leaves still pack a punch but are milder in flavour and softer in texture.

Mizuna

Of Chinese origin, mizuna has been cultivated in Japan for many centuries. Now it is slowly becoming almost as fashionable as rocket and is indeed similar. It too has a frilly leaf and a subtle peppery and vaguely mustardy flavour. Use mizuna in salads where you want good looks as well as substance.

Pak Choi

This is one of the favourite salad leaves being used in Pacific Rim cooking. Originally from China, this member of the cabbage family has delicately flavoured leaves which are attached to a crisp white stem. Also knows as Bok Choi, baby leaves can be steamed whole and dressed; larger leaves can be shredded and tossed in an oriental dressing of soy sauce, rice vinegar and a smattering of freshly chopped chilli.

DRESSINGS

Gone are the days when there were just two choices: salad cream or nothing at all. And instead of relegating olive oil to the shelves of the chemist's shop, it now takes pride of place in our kitchens, ready to adorn all sorts of salads. It is joined by many other types of fashionable oils and interesting vinegars, most of which are easily available. Although most oils should be kept in a coolish place (but not the refrigerator) and also preferably somewhere out of bright sunlight, they still have a fairly limited shelf life, particularly the nut oils. Most vinegars, provided they are kept in suitable conditions, will keep for ever.

Some of my favourite oils are **olive oil** (opt for extra virgin for the purest taste on your salads), **hazelnut, walnut, pumpkin seed** and **pistachio,** and of course **sesame oil** (used only in moderation) for a hint of oriental flavouring. I have also tasted a good **avocado oil** in South Africa and a superb, rich **macadamia nut oil** in Australia, but these are not yet widely available. For bland oils to make mayonnaise or to eke out the more expensive nut oils, my favourite is **sunflower,** but **groundnut oil** is also good.

As for vinegars, the darling of the restaurant trade is, of course, **balsamic vinegar** and a simple dish of sliced sun-ripened tomatoes needs little else but a drizzle of well-aged balsamic vinegar to make it into a feast. **Cider vinegar** and either **red** or **white wine vinegars** are the classics in traditional French dressings. **Herb vinegars** (**tarragon, thyme, basil** or **mint** are all suitable) add a little *je ne sais quoi* to your salad dressing, while **rice vinegar** lends an oriental touch.

One of my favourite vinegars is **sherry vinegar,** a good deal cheaper than balsamic vinegar but with a similarly rich flavour. It blends well with good olive oils to make a memorable and mellow dressing. I advise keeping distilled **malt vinegars** purely for making chutneys and pickles and not salads. But don't forget their primary role – dousing over a plate of shop-bought fish and chips.

Vinaigrette

*Once made, this can be
refrigerated in a screw-top jar
for a couple of days.*

1 tablespoon vinegar (balsamic,
wine or sherry)
½ teaspoon Dijon mustard
Coarse sea salt
Freshly ground pepper
Approximately 4–5 tablespoons
extra virgin olive oil

Mix the vinegar with the
mustard and seasoning in a
small bowl. Using a small
balloon whisk, whisk in
enough oil to give a thick
emulsion. Check seasoning
once more.

Mayonnaise

*If this shows signs of curdling, do
not hurl it all in the bin and go off
to weep as you count the cost of
your expensive ingredients.
Instead, drop in a whole ice cube
and whisk madly until it recovers
its glossy, creamy texture.*

2 medium free-range egg yolks
½ teaspoon Dijon mustard
1 teaspoon lemon juice
Salt and freshly ground black
pepper
300ml (10fl oz) oil
(I like half sunflower, half olive)

Place the yolks, mustard,
lemon juice and some salt and
pepper in a food processor.
Process for a few seconds, then
dribble in the oil – literally
drop by drop – in a slow but
steady trickle. Once an
emulsion has formed, increase
to a thin stream until all the oil
has been used. Tip into a bowl,
stir in ½ tablespoon of boiling
water, then season according
to taste.

Herb Dressing

*Use whichever herbs happen to
come to hand, but I would
recommend any of the following:
sweet cicely, bronze fennel,
chervil, flat-leaf parsley,
marjoram or mint. This is the
dressing to use on a summer
salad decorated with plenty of
edible flowers.*

1 tablespoon raspberry vinegar
2 tablespoons sunflower oil
2 tablespoons extra virgin olive
oil
2 tablespoons freshly chopped
herbs
Salt and freshly ground black
pepper

Place everything in a large
screw-top jar, season and
shake well.

Roasted Garlic Aïoli

Serve this with poached salmon, roast beef or a platter of lightly cooked summer vegetables such as potatoes, green beans, artichokes and broad beans.

3 large garlic cloves, unpeeled
Salt and freshly ground black pepper
¼ teaspoon Dijon mustard
1 medium free-range egg
1 tablespoon lemon juice
200 ml oil (7 fl oz) oil (I like half sunflower, half olive)
+ 1 extra teaspoon oil

Preheat the oven to 180°C/ 350°F/gas mark 4. Place the garlic cloves in a small ovenproof dish with the teaspoon of oil and roast for 20–25 minutes until tender. Remove from the oven and leave to cool.

Once cool, snip off the ends of each clove and squeeze the soft insides into a food processor. Add a pinch of salt, the mustard and egg.

Process for 20–30 seconds, then add the lemon juice. Process for a few more seconds, then, with the machine running, very slowly pour in the oils. You should have the consistency of a thinnish mayonnaise. Season to taste with salt and pepper and add extra lemon juice if necessary.

Thousand Island Dressing

This archetypal American dressing goes wonderfully with prawns, crab or any seafood.

200 g (7 oz) mayonnaise
40 g (1½ oz) tomato ketchup
2 teaspoons brandy
Dash of Tabasco sauce
¼ red onion, peeled, finely chopped
2–3 spring onions, finely chopped
1 heaped tablespoon fruity chutney
Salt and freshly ground black pepper

Stir everything together well and, if necessary, season to taste with salt and pepper.

Cranberry or Lingonberry Vinaigrette

Use this to liven up leftover roast turkey or chicken over the festive period.

1 tablespoon red wine vinegar
Salt and freshly ground black pepper
2 tablespoons cranberry or lingonberry sauce
2 tablespoons sunflower oil
2–3 tablespoons olive oil

Mix the vinegar with plenty of salt and pepper, then whisk in the sauce and sufficient oils to give a thickish emulsion with a pouring consistency. Season according to taste.

Chilli Vinaigrette

I like this vinaigrette served over bland winter root vegetables such as parsnips, celeriac, swede or potatoes. It also livens up many other salad ingredients from smoked fish to cold meats. When preparing chillies, do not rub your eyes – you'll make them sting.

2 red chillies, halved, deseeded
1 garlic clove, peeled
1 tablespoon sherry vinegar
4 tablespoons olive oil
Salt and freshly ground black pepper

Preheat the oven to 200°C/ 400°F/gas mark 6. Place the chillies and garlic in a small oven dish with 1 tablespoon of the olive oil and roast for 20 minutes, turning once. Remove, snip the chillies into small pieces and tip everything (oil and all) into a food processor with the vinegar and remaining olive oil. Whizz until processed, then season to taste with salt and pepper.

Pesto

Now as ubiquitous as ketchup, pesto adds oomph to pastas, stuffings, quiche fillings and, above all, to salad dressings. Make the consistency thinner than normal when dressing salads. This dressing freezes well.

50g (1¾oz) pine nuts
65g (2½oz) basil leaves
2 garlic cloves, peeled, crushed
50g (1¾oz) freshly grated Parmesan cheese
¼ teaspoon salt
125–150ml (4–5floz) olive oil

Preheat the grill and toast the pine nuts for 2–3 minutes. They can burn very easily so do keep an eye on them.

Place the cooled pine nuts in a food processor with the basil, garlic, Parmesan and salt then process until combined. With the machine running, slowly add sufficient oil to form a paste (thick for pasta, thinner for salads). Taste for seasoning and add if necessary.

Tapenade

As with pesto, thin this down with extra olive oil for salad dressings. Tapenade also freezes well.

350g (12oz) jar of black olives (Kalamata are good), drained well and stoned
2 garlic cloves, peeled, chopped
50g (1¾oz) tin of anchovy fillets, drained, chopped
5–6 basil leaves
2 tablespoons capers, drained well
1 rounded teaspoon Dijon mustard
The juice of ½ lemon
About 75ml (3floz) olive oil
Freshly ground black pepper

Place everything apart from the oil and seasoning in a food processor and process until blended. Then add the oil through the feeder tube – you will need enough to give a thinnish paste. Taste and add pepper if necessary (you probably will not need salt as the anchovies are quite salty). Cover and refrigerate.

Toasted Walnut Dressing

Serve this dressing over young leaves such as spinach, lamb's lettuce or baby sorrel.

50g (1¾oz) walnuts
2 tablespoons walnut oil
2 tablespoons sunflower oil
1 teaspoon Dijon mustard
The juice of 1 lemon
1 teaspoon honey
Salt and freshly ground black pepper

Preheat the grill and toast the nuts for 3–4 minutes until they begin to turn golden brown and you can just start to smell them. They can burn easily so do keep an eye on them. Allow to cool.

Place the oils, mustard, lemon juice and honey in a bowl, whisk together and season with salt and pepper. Stir in the walnuts just before tossing over the salad.

Horseradish Dressing

This is ideal with cold beef, smoked fish or prawns.

4 tablespoons olive oil
The juice of 1 lemon
2 teaspoons horseradish relish
Salt and freshly ground black pepper

Whisk together the oil, lemon juice and horseradish and season with salt and pepper, adding more horseradish if you like extra punch.

Blue Cheese Dressing

I recommend Stilton, Lanark Blue or Roquefort for this dressing which is lovely over frisée, with perhaps a few toasted walnuts or pecans and some slices of ripe pear thrown in.

50g (1¾oz) blue cheese, crumbled
2 tablespoons white wine or cider vinegar
3 tablespoons walnut or hazelnut oil
3 tablespoons sunflower oil
Dash of lemon juice
Salt and freshly ground black pepper

Process everything together in a food processor, adding just enough lemon juice to sharpen up the flavour. Add salt and pepper to taste.

INDEX